KEEP ME FLYING

John Ingram and Tom Ingram

Cover by: Martin Coven

ISBN: 979-8-9903877-0-6

10 9 8 7 6 5 4 3 2 1

Acknowledgments

Thank you to the Coven family, Martin, Ashley, and their daughter Riley for helping me with transcribing the letters. Also would like to mention that Riley came up with the title of the book.

Thank you to Chaplain Chuck Carlson for getting me thinking that I have a book that my Dad wanted to write.

Thank you to my Uncle LaMarr Ingram for the forward and for answering questions about family.

Thank you to Janet L. Zapata for the interview because without it I don't think I have a book.

Thank you to my sister Betsy and brother John for their help in keeping me from giving up on writing this book.

A special thank you to Brianna Castner for formatting this book and guiding me through the publishing process.

Table of Contents

FORWARD
BY LAMARR INGRAM

John Ingram was my brother but also my hero. While I was only 4 years old when he enlisted in the Army Air Corps I am reminded of the day he returned in the summer of 1945 and I welcomed him with the picture of me saluting his arrival.

I am reminded by the picture of the family story of the day of his arrival home by not telling anyone as to when he would return. He arrived by train to our town, took a cab to our home and had the driver drop him off a few blocks away. Our neighbor happened to be outside and saw him walking a few blocks to our home and ran to tell my mother of his arrival. The family welcomed him after two years of not seeing him and his arrival was documented with the picture of me saluting his return.

He was soft-spoken, a true southern gentleman and even the experience of his military service could not harden his newfound return to civilian life. It's been immensely gratifying to see his children, especially Tommy, take a profound interest in his wartime experience and carry his mettle. A blue star service flag, which represents a family member serving in the military, hung in the window of our home.

Since John was 14 years older than me I did not have a lot of contact with him during my formative years. He had gone to college, married and had two children while I was only entering middle and high school. I still looked up to him as my hero and attempted to follow in his footsteps by belonging to the Civil Air Patrol while in high school and had plans to enlist in the Air Force after college. I attempted to join the Air Force and I had passed the written test to qualify for enlistment but failed the physical due to my failure of the eye exam. I then joined the Navy and served my country as a tribute to my country and my brother in recognition of his service.

Today I am a volunteer at the National World War II museum in New Orleans in honor of my country and my brother's service as well. I want my grandchildren to know why those who served in World War II are rightfully called "The Greatest Generation" and about my brother John. Our family's goal is with this book to keep John's memory alive and pass on the greatness in the next generation.

LaMarr Ingram

PREFACE

My name is Tom Ingram. My family calls me Tommy. I am the son of John H. Ingram Jr. My father always wanted to write a book about his experiences in World War II. He never got around to doing it and died on December 19, 2008.

In 2018, I was coming back from a business trip and struck up a conversation with the gentleman sitting next to me on the plane. We started talking about our fathers and he became very interested when I told him that my father was a B-17 pilot in World War II and that he wanted to write a book about becoming a pilot. I told him that I had found an interview he did in 2002 and also the letters that he wrote to his parents when he left home to join the Army Air Corps. He said I needed to write the book for him using the interview and the letters. His name was Chuck Carlson and he is a Chaplain at Large in Arizona. Thank you Reverend Chuck for the inspiration and encouragement you gave me to do this for my father.

My father was interviewed on May 9, 2002 by Janet L. Zapata. She asked him various questions about his experiences and memories as a pilot in World War II. Janet sent him the transcript later that year and suggested he make any necessary corrections. I found it in his desk drawer after he had passed away and to my knowledge he never got back in touch with her.

The letters are the original post office letters that my father wrote to his parents when he left home after graduating high school to join the Army Air Corps. They were found by my brother at our grandparents house. They were still in the original envelopes in a chester drawer along with some old pictures. Even though my father did not keep a journal, these letters read like a journal and tell his story of becoming an Eighth Air Force pilot. I put them in chronological order starting when he left home in 1943 and ending when he returned home in 1945.

He ended some of his letters with "Keep Me Flying" so I feel he would have liked this for the title of his book.

This has been a labor of love putting his book together and I hope he would approve of the job I have done.

Thanks Dad, and Keep Flying!

Interview

May 9, 2002

By: Janet L. Zapata

INTERVIEW INTRODUCTION

I first met John Ingram through his lovely wife Mary. Mary and I vacationed at the same hotel in Rockport, Texas at the same time each year for many years. Mary was one of the friendliest, kindest, and most generous ladies I've ever had the joy to know. One day over lunch she mentioned that her husband John had flown bombers in World War II. At the time I was very interested in WWII and was especially intrigued by the experience of the airmen of the Mighty Eighth in the 8th Army Air Corps.

I had recently learned about the Veterans History Project where the Library of Congress was collecting veterans' recollections of their war experiences. I asked Mary if she thought John would let me interview him.

Mary talked to him and he agreed. Looking back over the interview, I see it wasn't much of an "interview." You can see that John had thought long and hard about whether or not he wanted to share his story and he knew exactly what he wanted to say. I didn't even have to ask many questions. John knew the story he wanted to get down on paper and he told it with very few questions from me.

Following the interview, I began the painstaking process of transcribing the tapes. I sat for hours on my computer hitting the start, stop, start, stop buttons on my cassette recorder until I finally had it all down on paper. I did the best I could to transcribe his story as he told it, but I was unsure if I had caught every word in every spot.

I sent the transcript off to John and asked him to review it and let me know of any changes he wanted to make. I remember having the feeling that I might never hear back from him with the changes. Somehow, I just knew he might not want to revisit that time again, and my instinct was right. He didn't send me any corrections and I waited about a year, and when I didn't hear from him, I packaged it up and sent it off to the archives of the Library of Congress and the original tapes and transcripts are there today.

John thought long and hard about whether or not he wanted to record what he and his fellow airmen had gone through. I believe he decided to speak of it all this one time and only this one time. After that he put the memories back in the drawer and never spoke of it again.

I believe that John was proud to have served his country and performed his duty. He had fun memories and great affection for the people he served with and the wonderful people of England that he came to know. But like my own father, who served in the Corps of Engineers during that time, he found nothing glorious about the war.

It was a great pleasure to know both John and Mary. May they rest in peace.

Janet Leach Zapata

Austin, Texas

Interview subject: John H. Ingram Jr.
Interviewed by: Janet L. Zapata
Interview date: May 9, 2002
Location of interview: Rockport, Texas
Transcribed by: Janet L. Zapata
Date transcribed: June 9, 2002

Zapata: These are the memories of John H Ingram Jr. who was born December 10, 1924. The interviewer is Janet Zapata. Mr. Ingram served in World War II. He was in the Army Air Corps and served in the 8th Air Force, ETO, 388TH Bomb Group and he was a 2nd lieutenant and served as a copilot on a B-17.

Ingram: Well, I thought I would start this thing with the fact that I did not keep a journal. Some of the guys did I'm sure and they have the dates and all of that in there. I wasn't interested in that, but anyway, in this interview as I'm recalling things, it's good to not be nailed down as to the dates and specific times of anything. I'm just off the top of my head trying to locate certain things that happened. Do you want to start off? Are you going to question me?

Zapata: You can go ahead and start and tell us a little bit about your background before the war.

Ingram: Pearl Harbor was on December 7, 1941. I was 16 years old. I was in the 11th grade at Durham High School in

Durham, North Carolina. Three days later I was 17 years old. On December 10, 1942, I was in 12th grade and immediately when you reached your 18th birthday you had to sign up for the draft. So, I signed up for the draft and they gave me a deferment to finish high school because I was a senior. The draft agency gave me a deferment to finish high school so I didn't have to go then. I knew I was going to have to go, just like the other kids at that age. They were leaving. Some of them would drop out of school, join up and volunteer. But I didn't, along with a lot of other people I'm sure because I wanted to finish high school. So I took the deferment and then I had time to think about what I wanted to do, how I wanted to go about this thing and If I had anything to say. In those days we didn't have much to say.

I was an aviation buff and I built model planes when I was a kid and I was in the aviation club in high school, so I wanted to fly if I could. They had lowered the standards. At my age when the war started you had to have at least a year of college. They had pretty strict standards, age, education and everything else, but as the war picked up, they lowered the standards because they got their production in tow and they needed people. So they lowered the standards and age limits and everything else. So I was able to qualify and take the written exam for the Army Air Corps. I think it was early '43. I took the written test and passed it.

That meant the next thing was the physical. And so in March of that year, they sent me to Seymour Johnson Air Force Base in Greensboro, North Carolina and I took the physical. And except for the blood pressure thing, which I told you about, it was pretty touch and go. I get nervous when they take my blood pressure and sometimes it's high. Because the last thing I think it was, they were taking my blood pressure and the old sergeant that was taking it walked in the room. He said John just lie there and relax and try to take a little snooze or something. I'll be back in a minute. And he left the room and was gone for maybe 5 or 10 minutes and anyway, he came back in and I followed his instructions and he took my blood pressure and that was it. So I passed. And I reflect on that a lot, because if I had flunked that blood pressure test, I don't know what would have happened. Every time they take my blood pressure now, I think of that. You know you get on in years and you think of the little things in your life that could have gone one way or the other depending on the little things. But anyway, I think of that. So I passed and they gave me my paperwork and said OK you're in. You will go back to your town and go with the draftees to Fort Bragg, when they ship you down there. Here is your paperwork. All you do is show them your paperwork. Because you're in. You just haven't been sworn in yet. So I did and sure enough the day after the last day of high school the bus was loaded down at the bus station with all the guys that had finished school. And there was a bus with two or three of us that had passed the Air Corps thing, with our paperwork.

They sent us to Fort Bragg and we went through the induction and the situation there with the draftees. And of course for me, it was just a walk-through. They looked at my papers and I just walked right on through. And when it was over, they swore in those that passed. They swore us all in the service, then told us to go back home and wait. They gave other guys a few days and then they would report somewhere. But since I was in the Air Corps, I thought I was going to go home and walk around town with those little cadet wings on my sweater for a good while. There were other guys in town that were in but hadn't been called yet. So I went to a house party, a senior house party down to the beach, and when I got back home after that week, I had the papers in the mail box to report to Biloxi, Mississippi. The papers had a certain date and a ticket on the train and everything else. So it didn't last long for me.

I went to Biloxi, Mississippi, to Keesler Field for basic training. I was only a wide-eyed 18-year-old kid who had never been over 150 miles away from home. They put you in fatigues and put you through basic training and that lasted about six weeks. That was mostly rifles and stuff like that, you know. They taught you to march and all that stuff and I was a long way from flying. When you finished basic training they sent us to what they called college training detachment. And looking back now, the pipeline was full of people who had volunteered and said, "I'll fly if you teach me how, and we'll go win the war." And they had the pipeline. They had everything set, but they had to get the training in, and so they had you in each little stage. You were put in that stage as they needed it, and if you didn't finish the curriculum, well they just pulled you out and shipped you on to the next stage.

So after basic training they sent us to Lubbock, Texas to Texas Tech. And there we took college courses, math and meteorology and things like that, and we also got a few hours of flying in a L-2A, which was out at an airfield in Texas near Lubbock. That is something like a piper cub. And of course it was all dual instruction, more or less, to just kind of orient you to it, I guess. It gave you an idea of what you would be looking at when you tried to learn to fly. Well anyway, I'll never forget this little thing that happened. My instructor was named Mr. Mayhew. He was a guy in about his 50's. My first real experience in a plane was when one day Mr. Mayhew said, "John, I'm going to put you in a loop now. I'll go through the motions and everything." He said, "You hold my grades." He had a grade clipboard he kept on his knee. And he handed me the grade clipboard and said to hold it and that was to keep it from flying and hitting anybody in the head or anything when we were at the top of the loop. And anyway, we started the loop and he was explaining, so many degrees nose down and you get up your speed and you start pulling gently back on the stick. And as he was talking, and about the first third of the loop, I was trying to see my grade. I was going to pick up that piece of paper and see how I was doing. And I couldn't pick the thing up because of the G's, you know, pulling you in the loop. But I will never forget the experience, because that was the first time I have really had some G's put on my body. I couldn't pick up the thing. Anyway, Mr. Mayhew was a nice guy and I remember him and I remember the time I tried to look at my grade and missed half of the instruction on how to do a loop. We didn't finish the curriculum at Lubbock and Texas Tech. But when they had room in the West Coast training command, eventually the order came down. They wanted so many guys put on the train and sent to Santa Ana, California for preflight. I think it was late September, maybe, because in the summer I was either traveling or in basic, and then I spent two or three months at Texas Tech. So this was fall of 1943.

So they sent us to Santa Ana, California for preflight. And here again you went through a physical. There were some that washed out there, but not too many to the best of my knowledge. If you passed that you were more or less in. Of course, anytime you didn't make the grade mentally, you were washed out. And that meant probably gunnery school. Most of the time it was gunnery school. So it behooves you to stay on the ball and do the right thing and work hard especially with kids like me with just a high school education. We had physics, certain things of physics. Of course I had physics in high school, but not anywhere near that. Anyway we started, and after I passed that I was in preflight in Santa Ana. Preflight was just general, more or less things like we took at Texas Tech, but the curriculum was already made out and you finished that, you didn't just get halfway through. And anyway preflight was the thing before you went to the flying stage. We finished preflight and then I was put with a group that went to Thunderbird Field in Phoenix, Arizona for primary flight training. And of course at that time, Phoenix was like 50,000 people and Thunderbird was out in the desert. But we were introduced to the Stearman PT-13. That was the two-wing trainer and that was the flying. The start of the flying training.

One of the things that preflight brings to mind is when you are an 18-year-old kid, you get homesick. But there are a lot of other guys along with you and you seem to pull together on taking care of that and other things. But at Christmas time in

Santa Ana, and I'll never forget this, I received a package like a lot of other guys. You got cookies and stuff like that from home and with mail call they delivered the packages and everything. I got a package. It was a pretty big package. I took it out to my bed, (sack) and set it on my footlocker like the other guys were doing. We were opening our packages and I opened this up and it was a Christmas tree with a note from my mom. And it said, "as a little boy, you liked Christmas trees." I was so embarrassed. It was smashed, you know, damaged in shipment, but the little bells and other things that were on there were OK. You couldn't set that thing up in the barracks. They wouldn't let you. You know you couldn't even have a sock out of place. And I was sitting there and I didn't know what to do with that little Christmas tree I had gotten. But I did. I snuck the thing downstairs and outside to the trash bin and threw it away. I got rid of it. But I'll never forget that. Moms are really a special thing.

Zapata: For the guys in the service, you think?

Ingram: Oh, yes, everybody. You didn't show it much because you were all manly you know. You couldn't show things like that. If it happened to you, you probably had too many beers or something and you got away with it. But I will never forget that Christmas tree. Opening that package and how shocked I was.

Zapata: Everyone was missing their moms?

Ingram: Oh yes. But I can't believe I was the only guy, I guess, who got a Christmas tree from his mom. I just couldn't believe it.

OK, where are we now? We are in Phoenix at Thunderbird Field. And they are teaching us to fly the PT-13 Stearman, which is a two-wing biplane you know. And that was really the fun part, one of the fun parts, to be able to get through primary training. Because we had airplanes that you really couldn't screw up in, why you could just get off the controls and if you have the altitude, it will come out by itself. But the big thing was soloing. And they only gave you about eight hours and if you didn't solo and your instructor didn't think you were ready and you hit eight hours, there were things done about it, I'm sure. So the program was to solo in that eight-hour period, which I did. And I'll never forget that day, we went to an auxiliary field, and Mr. Palance was my instructor. Again, a civilian instructor, George Palance. And he said, "OK John, I think I have done all I can do and this is it." And that was the time when I soloed. Just to know you can do it. And I took off and circled and landed and that was the solo. And that was the highlight of primary training. We went into rolls and loops and stalls and everything later on, which was good. You learn to get the feel of your body's reaction to certain positions of the plane and everything. I forgot how many hours we had. Anyway, that was when you bought a logbook at the PX and started logging your time and everything.

And that lasted about 15 hours and then you forget it, you know. That was the highlight of primary training in that little PT-13 that you could do just about anything in it and get away with it. You had loops and rolls and you could improvise and everything else and not worry about it if you had enough altitude, you didn't want to do things low. As I said, I forget how many hours we had in it, but that was the introduction to the flying part. And in Phoenix, Arizona the weather was good. This was early in the spring I guess. The weather was good. We weren't held up at all. We just got our time in, right on through there, no problem. There wasn't much leave time. You had Saturday at noon until Sunday afternoon, just overnight. Phoenix wasn't anything like it is now. That was the flying training, the first primary flying.

From there they sent us back to California, and, by the way, I was in the class of 43G. F or G, anyway, they went by numbers, and that was the class. So my class was shipped to California to Cal Aero, which was another civilian flight school that had civilian instructors. And it was a nice place. I was very fortunate to be in the West Coast Training Command because you had some good places to go, or at least I thought anyway. Cal Aero was in Ontario, California, right out of LA and it was a civilian base. We didn't have to stay in barracks. We were in private facilities, we had suite mates and things like that. We had two to a room and a bath between the other room. The accommodations were great, the food was great and we flew the BT-13. The basic trainer was a canopy thing, with a fixed landing gear and I think a 450 horse engine or something like that. It was a real airplane compared to the Stearman. They are the highlight there.

One thing I remember is that I was on cross-country one time, flying the BT-13. I was on the last leg of the cross-country back to the base and the engine started acting up, it sputtered and so I went to the wobble pump. The wobble pump is a pump you do by hand when you start the engine, to get fuel pressure up. You use the wobble pump, that was the procedure. So, when I hit the wobble pump, it straightened out and I kept going. Well anyway I don't know how far it was, I stayed on the wobble pump and flew that thing all the way back to the base. And when I got there, I made the best landing I ever made in a BT-13, wobbling on that pump. I felt really good about it. I was at an airshow in Houston not long ago and they had a BT-13 out there and I asked them if they would let me look up there and see the wobble pump. And he said, "There it is, the red handle right over there on the left." But things like that, was your first real thing, and I said uh-oh, things can happen you know. It could've been the fuel in it or something, I don't know. But anyway, she was acting up. And that's the thing to do, to hit that wobble pump and it came out of it and I got home alright in it. And we wrote it up on the form. And that was about it for basic. Except you had the canopy, the slide canopy, you did a little formation flying, and you did night flying, which was new.

Oh, and another thing in basic, we were not supposed to get above the cloud cover. You are not supposed to get out of sight. You were supposed to be able to land all the time. You don't get above the weather, the clouds. One day, I was up by myself and it was partly cloudy and there was a hole in the clouds. And I said I've never seen what it looks like to get up on top of the thing. So I just thought to myself, I will go up through the hole and look around and come back down. So I did. I sneaked up through the hole and got on top and it was awesome! You could see the cloud cover and everything and I could see Old Mount Baldy over there, which is a checkpoint for our base. And when I got through it and all in, I started spiraling down through that hole in the cloud and all of a sudden I saw a plane coming up right on me. And I mean it was just right there. And it momentarily scared me. I jerked and got through it and then I realized, that's my shadow! The sun was behind me and that was my shadow. And, you know, it looks just like a plane coming at you. Like looking in a mirror, you know? And I panicked for a minute until I realized that was my shadow. I mean that's not another plane. These are the little things you remember, you know you didn't want to admit that. I never told anybody. I didn't think we told anything that was out of line, because they could report you and you weren't supposed to do that.

And another thing, one day I was doing a little practicing because I had a check ride the next day. And in that check ride, I was going to get what they call maximum turn. Anyway, your check pilot or instructor would give you a turn, it was a chandelle more or less. You pulled up and got maximum altitude of your climb, turning climb, without stalling out. It teaches you the limits of the plane and everything. I was practicing my maximum turns which I was going to get on the next day's check ride. I had gotten out of my area evidently, and next to us was El Toro, the

Marine base over there in California and they would fly the Navy's F6F, something like that. And evidently, I was out on the edge of our territory. I don't think I was out of our territory, because you had territory you were supposed to stay in. Well, some Marine pilot saw this little kid flying an airplane, so he drove over me and I was in my maximum turn and I looked and I could see that oval shape cowling of the F6F and it was coming head on. It scared the bejesus out of me. I rolled it over and afterwards, you know I thought he saw me and he said, I'll just scare the guy's butt off. And he dove over and right head on. Of course it was dangerous, but they did things like that. Everybody thought the more reckless you were the better, but they changed that. But anyway, he scared the heck out of me. And that was it for basic training. We had good quarters, good airplanes, maintenance was good, and the time off with LA in the area was great. It was just a good place for that particular part of it.

OK, we got basic flying training with the Vultee BT-13 Valiant. And the next stage was the advanced training and that was the summer of '44. I was in a unit that was sent to Fort Sumner, New Mexico. And this was the only Army base that I trained at, where there were Army instructors, Air Corps instructors, you know Army everything. This was the only one. The others were civilian bases, civilian instructors, etc. Of course we had Army personnel there for the cadre you know, but this was the first Army pure thing. It was out in the middle of nowhere, Fort Sumner, and we flew a twin-engine trainer. Of course, when you got through, when you finished that stage of flying training, we had a little thing you filled out and you put your preference of what you wanted to do, what you wanted to fly. And so, my preference was P-38s. I was very impressed with the P-38 because in California they had a training thing that was near our area and it was the P-38 that would go up, especially in the afternoon, about four o'clock. They would go through their things and you could see them from our field. The instructors would have you follow the leader. The instructor would take off and do everything and you were supposed to stay on his tail, stay right with him. It was just beautiful to just stand there and watch those P-38s operate. And I wanted to fly a P-38, so I put down multi-engine fighters, twin-engine fighters, that's a P-38. Maybe that was my demise, because I got multi-engines, but I didn't get the fighter end of it. So I got instead the UC-78, that's what we call the Bamboo Bomber. It was a training plane, a twin-engine training plane and that was the advanced training up in Fort Sumner, New Mexico. You just did mostly flying because you have plenty of room and nowhere to go on the weekends. We had army instructors. My instructor, his name was Rodriguez, and I can remember that.

And oh yeah, we were night flying and I was in a Bamboo Bomber. You had a pilot and a copilot. I was flying the left seat, the pilot, and my copilot, named Ingold, was in the right seat. When you went through training you went alphabetically you know. You roomed with H, I, J. But anyway, Ingold was my copilot that night. And I took off. We were shooting landings, night landings in the Bamboo Bomber. And on my down leg, downwind leg, the instruments started going out. The instrument lights were going down. I turned on my basic leg and lowered the wheel, lowered the landing gear. And then of course the procedure was to look out. I've got wheel, the copilot would say, I got wheel. And you looked because the wheel extended from the engine itself. Anyway, to make a long story short we had electrical failure. And that was mechanically. That was why my instrument lights were going dim and everything. So when we hit the wheel switch, the wheels probably extended but they didn't extend full-length. They were about halfway. And on that particular airplane when you had full extension of your landing gear, you pulled a metal cable, you pulled the switch down there, and it locked your wheels in place from the landing gear. Anyway, when I came in on the approach and whipped the problem of electrical failure, never knowing that my wheels were not fully extended. Anyway, when I landed it, when I pulled back on the stick and landed it, the landing gear collapsed. And of course it started turning, the right tire blew and we started turning in on the ground slide on the runway and it was turning into that little blown tire. and I stood up on the left brake. Anyway, we stopped the turn and skidded on down the runway and then we were both out of there because of fire. The Bamboo Bomber would go up in flames in a minute, but it didn't. There was no fire or anything. But it was an accident, and to make it worse, I was worried. I said uh-oh, here I am in the last of the thing and this thing has to happen. And I went through it that night when I got in the sack and I thought about everything. And I said, no I did the right thing all the way through. So anyway, the next day, I was called before the engineering department, the investigative thing of the Army. They got my side of the story and they, in turn, had the plane inspected and had a report on the plane. Of course I sweated it out all day long, but when it was all over, they said you did what you were supposed to do. You went through the right procedure and you were just lucky the thing didn't catch fire. And so I didn't wash out but that was close. I was afraid I would be washed out of that stage of the game. And man we were just weeks from graduation. But they considered it mechanical failure. That particular airplane, the Bamboo Bomber, was all electrical. There were no hydraulics on it. It was all electrically done. The landing gear was electric motors that lowered the landing gear with a screw effect thing, and the flaps were electric, everything was electric on there. And if you lost your electrical system, why that's like a dead battery or a battery going out, I guess. And you just lose everything, and that's bad, especially at night. In the daytime I can see, you could actually manually crank your gear down. If it happened in the daytime, you could always see your instruments. You could lower your flaps mechanically or land it without flaps. And your gear, there was a procedure where you could crank them down with a crank, manually. But since we looked and both of us assured each other that we had a gear, we could see it. We could see the wheel, but it wasn't all the way down. So that is when it collapsed.

Well where are we now? We finished advanced flying training and anyway we graduated. Then I went home on leave. That was the first time I had been home since I went into the service. The next station was Las Vegas, Nevada. Where we had the copilot training or the pilot training on the B-17. But anyway that was the first introduction to the B-17. And I reported out there in the summer of '44, and that was a Las Vegas Army Air

Base and a gunnery training school. Because we had gunners in the B-17s and we also had pilot training in the B-17s. And this was for copilots because the first pilots had a more extensive training earlier and more of it. They were probably already in their training areas and phases and probably finished it. And Roswell had a big transition base. Anyway, the Las Vegas thing was the introduction to the B-17. And we flew gunners on gunnery ranges and other than flying, the Air Corps was doing two things. It was training gunners and also introducing the pilots to the B-17. And that was a short thing. I don't know how many weeks we were there. But Las Vegas was nothing like it is now. It was pretty good duty because the weather was good. The scenery was awesome. The program was pretty good because you just learned the airplane.

From there we were sent to Tampa, Florida. I had leave time before going to Tampa. I went home and then was to report to Tampa, Florida. It was Drew Field in Tampa, Florida. That was early fall of '44 I think. And Tampa was where the crew was formed. Ten men were put together. A pilot and a copilot, navigator, bombardier, engineer, radio operator, and the gunners. You were assigned a crew and that was when the training started. It was a good place to train, it was scenic. I was on a crew with a pilot that was a 25-year-old man, who was married and had a kid, I think one or two kids. I was the copilot. The navigator was a 27-year-old man who was married and had a child or two. And he had his wife with him down there. She and the bombardier were like a year older than I was, or he might have been the same age. George, our bombardier, was from the coal mines in West Virginia. He was a neat guy. That was the four officers in the crew. The engineer was a guy from Fort Worth, Texas. He was also the top turret gunner. The radio operator was a fellow from South Carolina. And the ball turret gunner was from Oregon, I think. The tailgunner was a Jewish guy, 19 years old. He was the youngest of the whole crew. That's not right, I was 19 and I wasn't 20 until December 1944. So I was 19 when we formed the crew and he was 19. So we were the two youngest. The navigator was an instructor. He instructed in navigation school in Louisiana.

We were going like mad over there in the war and we take these guys who have been trained already here and we need more. We got the airplanes. They were making them as fast as they could. We're getting the equipment. We've got the men, and we've got the materials. Looking back now, you could see the logistics of the thing was to man those heavies and get there. And if we have to go into the training area and pick up instructors or send somebody to replace him, we will do it. Because looking back now at the logistics in the war like that, it's absolutely mind-boggling. You've got to have everything in line and a back up plan too, I guess. So that's the way we trained as a crew. And in that training you were working together. The gunners shot targets in the bay, Tampa Bay. They didn't have any sleeve training. The sleeve training for gunners was out in Las Vegas. That's when they fired at the sleeve towed by an airplane, usually a P-38, P-39, or a P-63 King Cobra. They had some women flying them out there, towing those targets. The B-26 also towed targets, and the women ran the pursuit curves on the airplanes coming at us and the gunners shot film, photographs. And they were graded on that too. But I remember those WASP's, the women pilots. We were kind of awed at that too. But they did a good job. They would fly pursuit curves at the formation and the gunners would shoot them with film instead of real ammo. The sleeve things were the ones that they shot real ammo at. Where am I now? Oh, Tampa, Drew Field. We train there and Tampa is a nice place, a nice place to train. I think advanced was the only real place where I was fortunate to get a lot of good training. And at Tampa, we put the crew together and we trained together and the next thing was to be shipped overseas.

From Tampa, after we finished the training, they sent us to Savannah, Georgia, to Hunter Field. And there we were supposed to pick up a new airplane. They were bringing the planes down from Michigan or wherever they built them, and bringing them to Savannah and then we would pick up those planes and supposedly we would fly them overseas. And of course we would be briefed on how to do that. It was just a bunch of crews there waiting for that and doing nothing. The program was for you to pick up this airplane and fly it over either by the northern route or the southern route. The northern route was Savannah, up to Goose Bay, Labrador, and then over to Iceland. But anyway, that was the northern route. You took off to Goose Bay and Bangor, Maine and places like that. But Goose Bay was the first stop, I think. The southern route took you down close to the Azores maybe. But anyway, there was a northern route and a southern route. But in our situation we never did get an airplane. Because the order came down that we were one of the ten crews and were sent to New York and put on the Queen Elizabeth, the biggest ship in the world. We were put on the train and sent up there. A hundred of us guys, which was ten crews. They had room on the boat and they said, OK we got room here and send us what you've got. And I still believe from the feedback that we were graded as a crew too. How would you pick ten crews to go like that? They would look at your marks or something. Anyway, I think we were pretty high on their priority list, because we were one of the ten crews. And the rest of them could stay there for months and when the war ended six months later, they were still there waiting, some of them. Those that flew the planes over, they were in weather up at Goose Bay. The word was, you get to Goose Bay and you're liable to sit there for a week and a half or two weeks until the weather breaks. And some of them, it could take them weeks to fly those airplanes because of the weather. And here we were, we were sent priority, I guess right to New York, put on Queen Elizabeth and that was an awesome thing. I mean it was just like walking into a building. You didn't even know you were on a ship. And in three-and-a-half days we were in Scotland. The Queen Elizabeth went by itself, no, we were escorted out of New York Harbor. I remember that. And from then on it was all by itself. And it ran a zigzag course for subs, I'm sure. But it was a fast ship and could out run the subs. I think they had to be in perfect position to get a shot off.

Zapata: Do you remember your last sights in New York?

Ingram: No, but I do remember we went to the club with the zebra striped seats in it. That was a famous nightclub up there. And other than that, we were on a schedule. And in three-and-a-half days, as I said I was on the Queen Elizabeth, going up the fjord in Scotland. And as I said, we were escorted to start with but then we were on our own. We were a day out of Scotland and that morning we had a Corvette, an English Corvette on each side of us. That was an English Destroyer. We also had a B-24 circling us. And that was our escort in the Firth of Clyde Fjord that you went into Scotland. And I remember we were under the British command, because it was a British boat. And under the British command officers ate in the dining room with tables and a white tablecloth and all that stuff like you're in a restaurant, and the enlisted men, they got to stand in a chow line down in the bottom of the boat all stacked up. We were housed in state rooms. And you talk about some real griping. All four of us officers were up there living the big time and our gunners were down there in vomit and everything else. They were down there and had to stand in a chow line and eat on their laps and it was also loaded with infantry down there. The infantry and the parachute guys. It was unbelievable, they were triple-loaded and in some instances they sat down eight hours and you stood up eight hours and you slept there eight hours. They rotated and it was triple-loaded.

And another thing I remember, I was made a loading officer. I was assigned a certain room or area and when the guys reporting to that area got on the ship, I was to make a speech and

give them the rules and regulations. How we were going, what
was going to happen, what they could do, and what they couldn't
do and all that. Just a speech you know. And then after that, I
was supposed to go back and check on them every once in a
while, in the course of the three days, because I was the loading
officer. As it turned out my bunch came in, and they were the
100th and the 82nd airborne. Some of them were going back for
the second time. They had already jumped on D-Day and
everything. And you were talking about some bitter people. I got
up there to make that speech and you should have heard the
booing and saying, get out of here. I was a young 20-year-old and
I thought, man, this is it, we're getting into the grungy part now.
Here are these guys stacked on top of each other, the bunks were
lined up on the walls, and just slam full. And some of these guys
were going back for the second time. They had also brought
drink on the boat in their duffel bags, they had bottles in there.
They had just enough clothes in there to keep the bottles from
breaking, I guess. But anyway, I went back one time to check on
them and that was the last time. I said, I'm not going to be a part
of that, the heck with it. But from then on things moved pretty
fast. You're thinking, you know you train and you get ready and
everything because when you get on that starting line things
move fast. You're thrown into things that you had no idea. You're
treated differently, I mean, you're just meat. And let's go, let's get
it. What you do and learn to do and now we're going to do it.
And they're going to put you in it as fast as they can. So I'll never
forget that, those paratroopers that were in there. And how they
were stacked in there. I will never forget how guilty you felt with
our gunners down in the hole there. And I don't know how many

that ship held, but it was in the thousands. Because that was during or right after the Battle of the Bulge or something anyway, it was late December or early January. It was in the winter of '44-'45. And they were throwing everything at them, and you know Patton was moving and so it was triple-loaded.

We got to Scotland and the boat dropped anchor. We went through some subnets too, I remember that. I remember the escort we had out at sea and then going up the fjord because it's scenic and when we got to where we anchored, there was no dock. The boats came out and took us off the Queen Elizabeth and took us into the dock. We didn't go into a slip or anything. The boat was hardly stopped, it was dragging anchor when the other boats from the shore were ready to move the infantry. Those infantry guys and paratroopers were the number one priority. We were, to my knowledge, the last ones to get off the boat. And of course when it came our time, they unloaded us and we rode the boat over to the shore and they put us on a train. You still didn't know where you were going. We rode the train all night long down to our station, which is a good ways from Scotland to go all the way down to East Anglia, where the Air Corps was. You don't remember much about that because it was in the dark. I do remember the priorities of how they unloaded us, The infantry guys and then my guys. Most of us didn't know what was going on, we just followed. You look back and you see how it was all laid out and the job that the top guys did on logistics and everything and it's just a real knack, I mean, our people did a good job there, as opposed to the enemy who was fighting on two fronts and all screwed up. And you can imagine one guy running the whole show, which was Hitler and he turned down things and he didn't approve this and he moved guys around and everything and they were fighting all over there. And I think we just had better people in that period of time. I don't know how they did it. To stand up to all the stuff they had to go through and then when the invasion came down. But that was it for getting there.

We were assigned to the 388th Bomb Group. Now, what happened to the other crews I don't know but we and maybe another two or three crews were assigned to the 388th. All the ten crews were not assigned to the same bomb group. I don't know which went where, but I know our crew was assigned to the 388th Bomb Group in Knettishall. I think they called it Station 136, or something like that. There are a lot of numbers you go by and that was more or less army lingo I guess. The 388th was in the 3rd Division. There were three divisions in the Eighth Air Corps. The 1st and the 3rd were B-17s and I think the 2nd was the B-24s, the ones with the funny looking tail. We were in that section or the area of East Anglia which is in east England. And we were jammed in there with airfields all over the area, so close to each other that you had to be careful about traffic patterns overlapping into other areas.

We are assigned a base now, the 388th in Knettishall. Our quarters were in Quonset huts and I think there were 16, four crews, but only the officers. Sixteen guys in a Quonset hut that made four airplane crews in that one hut. It was a little metal building with bunks and a little coke stove at one end of the building. The stove was no bigger than a nail keg and you were rationed coke which is coal charcoal. You put the coke in there and burned it. Coke burns pretty hot, you know. One end of the hut stayed too hot, and the other end was cold. And of course it was the winter of '44-'45, and it was cold. And the next thing was the practice missions. We were not assigned an airplane. They had a pool of planes, but I don't know how many it consisted of. There were guys going home or had gone home. They had finished their missions, their tour, and we were replacements naturally. We were to fly what we had. So we were assigned planes and you never once had one plane. We flew a couple of practice missions to get the feel of the area and everything.

Our airfield was in a farming section, full of sugar beet farmers. The US filled it with barracks, runways, and taxiways and things like that. And we paid those farmers for the beets they couldn't raise. They raised sugar beets in between the runways, anywhere there was land, they plowed it. So you were taking off and landing while looking out and the farmer had his big old draught horses and was plowing and raising sugar beets. In the air fields out there everything was dispersed for safety reasons to keep some German from dropping one bomb and blowing up the whole area. The mess hall was dispersed, the flight lines were dispersed, headquarters was in one place, but the quarter areas weren't as dispersed as much, but still they were a good ways off. So you had to walk. So consequently, the first thing you did was to buy a bicycle. And you bought bicycles from the guys that were leaving and these were the English bicycles, which were just the necessities, the bare things. It didn't have anything like the balloon tires or anything like what we had. But anyway you bought a bicycle. You ride your bicycle to the mess hall and to the flightline. You very seldom walked from one place to the other, except for your own squadron area. So that was your transportation. We also rode the bicycles into town and to church. We would ride them to the little pubs, because this was all a rural area, and the bicycles were our transportation. It was almost a necessity. It was a luxury and an expense and we had plenty of them too. And let's see, the next was the practice missions. We flew a couple of practice missions, I think. I know we practiced missions, but how many, I don't know. And they were up in the area. Some of them went up to Scotland and back and since it was winter time the weather was the main thing. Weather had a lot to do with whether we went on a mission or not. Not only weather in the field and at the area, but over into Germany and France and places. So weather in the wintertime was a big thing for the flying bunch.

I am trying to recall all of this because like I said, I didn't take a journal or anything. The first mission was to Hanover, and I know our disappointment when we got out to the airplane. Of course you had your briefing. You got up at 3:30-4:00 o'clock in the morning. Let me back up a bit, at the officers club they had a light over the bar. And there was a red light and a green light. If the green light was on, that means that we stood down. Nothing scheduled or anything, and you could get a drink which was gin and juice. But when the red light was on over the bar, they had a list. The list was right outside and if you were up and scheduled for a mission the next day, you didn't drink or anything. You go home and go to bed. You don't partake of the officers' club things.

I told this to a little girl in our hometown newspaper and I remember she wrote it up, and I was really embarrassed about this thing. When you read it you think that we just sat down. Everybody sat in one room and watched for the light to turn red or green. That wasn't the case, you know. It was just a thing there, for the bartender and everyone. If you were up for a mission, you looked on the schedule to see if your crew was on it or not. If not, OK I will serve you a drink but if you are, you don't get anything. You go home and go to bed.

As I said our first mission was to Hanover. After briefing we went out to the ship, the airplane that was assigned to us. And two things that I remember about it was in the briefing they sighted our crew that we would have the mail and we didn't know what the mail was, but it turned out the mail was the propaganda sheets. We didn't have any explosives on the airplane at all. They put in sheets of propaganda and they would flood the towns with the sheets that we hit and they would flutter down. So we were a little disappointed, you know. But looking back now we were darn glad. I also remember that in the first mission, it was a continental assembly. They didn't do this very often but if the weather was so bad for so long and they needed to get something done, they would schedule a continental assembly. Ordinarily you would take off and form over your field, and after you got your group formed, then you would strike out for the target and go across the English Channel. I don't know how many of these continental assemblies they did, but we did it on this mission. I don't know, but it might have been the first continental assembly in the history of the war. Anyway, in a continental assembly you

take off in individual ships and fly to France. In France, right
north of Orly Field, Paris, there was a buncher. A buncher is a
radio station, with a tower and the buncher sends out a signal
and you see it on a map, it has four legs to it. We took off in
individual sequence and flew individually over the channel to
this buncher. And when we got to it, we had a procedure.
Everybody was forming over that, and our group was forming
over that too. We took off in the soup, it was messy flying, I mean
on instruments and everything. When we got to the buncher we
would be forming and our group would be firing a yellow flare.
I'll never forget our CO, he was an old guy, I won't call his name,
but he said, "I'll be faring yeller flowers in the air." And that
meant he's the lead ship in the group and that's the squadron you
tail into. But I'll never forget that. I thought gah, we got a pig
farmer for a CO. Coming up on the buncher, we were still in the
soup. We couldn't see anything, and then all of a sudden it started
clearing and according to Jake, our navigator, we were coming
into the buncher like we were supposed to be. We looked out
and it was just clear, and sure enough there were the "yeller
flowers" in the air, and there were a few ships that had already
fallen into formation and we just tagged right in. It was just
unbelievable, and it worked out anyway. It was some kind of,
sorry, I'm choking up! Our group was circling and we had the
flares right there and we just made a short right turn and fell right
into the slot where we were supposed to be. There was a sigh of
relief from everybody. We were observing strict radio silence as
far as talking to other ships. We talked among ourselves, but it
was neat the way that all the crap we went through going over
there to the buncher and then just all of a sudden it was so clear.

And going back to briefing we had a young guy who was our weather officer and he had a speech in the briefing and they would introduce him and we would all boo him because of the weather. It isn't like that now. We can nail down anything about the weather. The weather was the biggest danger with flying, even today.

Well anyway, after we formed, we struck out for our target area. I don't know how far that is from the buncher, but we got to the target area, the initial point, the IP as we called it, and then we went into our formation of leveling up and spreading out. You had to, the group was like four squadrons of 12 planes each and they were all staggered, and if you look at pictures you see there was a high element, a low element, a high squadron, and a low squadron. When you got to the IP, you went in squadrons, which is three or four, and you lined up behind each other. You still kept your squadron formation, except instead of flying the low and the high and the slot area, you pulled up to the same elevation and leveled out. You were all at the same height. And then you were down in the bomb run. And that day we were bombing by instrument, which is Gee Box and Mickey. That was the name for it. I remember the song we used to sing down there. I bombed Cologne with my Mickey and Gee Box to guide me. It was to the tune of "I Walk Alone", you said "I Bombed Cologne." And anyway, we started down the bomb run, leveled up, strung out like we were supposed to do, and everything was fine, except I looked up and we were going into the area and there was nothing but big black smoke. We didn't know anything about anti-aircraft fire. What you learned was from the guys next to you in your barracks area. They didn't tell you anything. When you see that red flash that means you're too close. If you just see the puff of smoke, you're OK. Don't worry cause you'll get some shrapnel. If you get it, it would be like throwing rocks and gravel against the airplane, but if you see that flash, you are too close. I looked up the bomb run and there was a bunch of smoke and in a situation like that, the Germans were using their anti-aircraft 88 guns, which they would guess or calculate your altitude and your heading and where you will probably be when you drop the bombs, when you toggle them on the target. And they would take that area and just fill it full of flack. To avoid it you would have to go around it or something, and then you screwed up the whole bomb run. So the only thing you could do is just hold tight and just fly right on into it. And if they got one, why it was luck. There was a name for it called boxing you, or something like that. But anyway they filled the area full of anti-aircraft, no fighters. I didn't see one fighter. To my knowledge there was not even one reported in the area. If fighters were reported we had cover. We had P-51s flying cover at that stage of the war. But in that bomb run there was this flak area or dark area with smoke. I learned later on that the lead and the deputy lead airplanes, ships, when they toggled or when they released the bombs they had a smoke bomb that went with it. And that was in case the bombardiers or the bomb group behind you screwed up or something went wrong with them, and their lead ship with the bomb, the guy on the bomb site, got shot down or something happened, you were not supposed to abort the mission at all. You just kept going and toggled on those trails of smoke. I looked up there and when they released in front of us, way up in front of us, there were trails of smoke and they looked just like in the movies. In the movies, you know in the old World War I movies, when they shot down a plane you had a trail of smoke going down. And I thought to myself, oh Lord, they have already shot down four or five of us guys up there in front of us. And I said, there ain't no way we can get through this. We are just going to be lucky if we get through this, and that's when you scooch down. You got your flak helmet on and you had a flak vest and you kind of scooch down. It might not do any good but I guess it helps. But anyway we made it through there and did our thing and made our turn and came out of it.

And to this day, I still think, why didn't they tell us? Nobody said anything because you don't. You're just taking one minute at a time and more or less learning. But I always thought that they should take the new crews, the ones that were replacing another crew that had gone home, and sit us down in a room and say OK guys, you know this is what we are going to do. Instead of leaving it up to briefing. Because in the briefing everybody is supposed to know the score. All you do is just get where you are going, altitude, all the specifics, what you are hitting, a ball bearing plant or a railroad station. They give you the specifics and don't give you anything else, because all these guys, most of the guys, are all experienced men. They have done that, but these first time guys they don't know what's going on. So I thought that was very much the thing that needed to be done. But naturally that's the way I saw it. If somebody would have just told me that the smoke bombs were carried on the leads and deputy leads and that was in case we could not see the target and we were bombing through the clouds and in bad weather. You might have to use it that day. But anyway it's a scary thing. And you never know, you sit in that ship and you figure out if something happens how in the heck am I going to get out of here. I would practice in my mind at night in the sack. First off, I take off my oxygen thing, headphones and everything, because you were tied to that ship. Then I can roll to my left, because we had to go down and through the trap and go out the front end of the plane. And if it's in a spiral or something like that you're in bad shape, because how are you going to move? And it's just all those things that you think of. If something happens and I've got time to get out of there, how will I do it? Will I panic then and mess up? And those are the things that go through your mind when you're back home and off the mission and you go through the debriefing. And then we usually sat around the little old coke stove back there and rehashed the mission. Of course, if it was a particularly rough one, there wasn't much said around there. And we were at the end of the war, and weather, flak, or screw ups could've got us. I never saw a fighter, a German fighter. We had P-51 cover, little friends. But there were times when fighters were reported in the area. When you put up 1,000 or 1,200 bombers and four or eight hundred fighters, it was just like a race track into Germany. You'd be going in and guys would be coming out. That went on all day long and at night the British were up there. So I don't know how those people took it. They couldn't take it. You had guys going in and when you got into an area in Germany, everyone had different targets. You went to a certain area and then you broke off and you went over here and hit this and another group went over there and hit that, and of course all of that came out in the briefing. You have primary targets and secondary targets. If something happened to your primary target, your bombsight went out or you screwed up over there or something happened, if there was a call for it, you had a secondary target. You went to the next target. It was just all day long. It was going in and coming out.

We finished up with the first mission which was Hanover and that was a completely new experience and I've covered that. The missions afterwards I don't remember every one of them. Some of them were eventful and some of them were not. The ones that I remember eventful were Munich and Dresden and I guess the last one was Karlsbad and those stand out in my mind right now. Munich stands out because it was the roughest mission that we flew. We lost two ships. We lost our wingman who was hit by flak between engines one and two, at least that's what our crew that saw it said and he went over the top of us. He didn't crash into us because he was flying off our wing. He went over us. I didn't see that because my head was in the instrument panel and on the control column flying. We also lost a slot man, Hogie, who they said was hit in the nose and that was a rough one as far as I'm concerned. On that particular mission was when I tell the story about the chewing gum. You would chew gum to keep your ears open until you got on oxygen. You chewed gum to keep your ears open and popping. And then I would take my chewing gum out and put it on the control column, right on that little cap that saysB-17 on the control column. And then hours later when you are coming home and you were low enough to get off oxygen, I would take my chewing gum off that little cap on the control column. That day we didn't make our usual turn to get out of the flak area. We kept going into the black area or the flak area, which was shown in briefing, and we had lost two ships already, and things weren't working out and I looked down and my chewing gum had come off the control column. It had frozen and somehow it came off and of course when things like that happened, you think well, this is it, we're not doing what we're supposed to have done and I lost my gum and that's my good luck charm. You feel the little red hot streak run down your esophagus and there's a sense of fear. And that was the one we made it out of and finally got back. I remember the Munich raid because of my chewing gum and losing those two ships. We were so close to our wingman who was just flying off our wing, that flak could have gotten us so easily. It was just a matter of 20 yards or less. But anyway, Munich I remember that, and it was a rough one.

Another one I remember was Dresden. That one sticks out because of the long haul down there. It was probably one of the deepest missions that I flew and when we got there the smoke from the fires from the night before when the British had hit it had risen to our altitude. We were going in at 20,000 feet. Of course later I have read books about it, read it was a holocaust to incinerate a whole city like that. The smoke had made it awfully difficult for us because the smoke had risen to our altitude. I remember we were ordered to drop down 2,000 feet, I believe it was. We dropped from 20,000 down to approximately 18,000 to get a better bomb run out of it. And not only that, there was a lot of confusion because there was another group coming in from our right, about two o'clock and that wasn't supposed to happen. You always were lined up, you never flew different headings on a bomb run. They were always behind each other. We looked over and there was a group coming in from our right. Maybe we got into the problem when we dropped down 2,000 feet, I don't know. But anyway, it was pretty much a touch and go thing. Of course, combat is controlled mayhem or uncontrolled mayhem, so you're lucky when you get out. We finished the mission and got back out of there without any losses. I remember our target, our primary target, was the central train station. We were briefed that there were military soldiers on the trains, people moving through and we just clobbered it. I think Dresden was Bomber Harris' answer to Coventry. If you remember Coventry when the Germans burnt Coventry down that was a holocaust, and supposedly this was the British who wanted to get back for the destruction of Coventry. Of course Dresden was full of artworks and architecture that could never be replaced, and they just wiped it out. It was terrible.

Let's see, I got Dresden, but of course there's Berlin and Hamburg. Berlin was taken off our list. I forgot what date it was, but in the briefing we were told that Berlin had been taken off because of the Russians approaching and everything. Thank goodness Berlin was taken off because it would've been pretty bad because of the flak guns. It probably had more anti-aircraft guns around the town than any other city because the Germans were retreating and pulling back their 88s and it was just full up. The other guys said when they say Berlin in the briefing you just sunk down in your seat. But that day they announced it had been taken off the list. There was a big cheering section, the guys stood up and hollered and as a green crew we didn't know, but we hollered along with them.

So Berlin was taken off the list and we didn't have to go and probably the next one that stood out was Kiel. We hit the sub pens in Kiel and that was a long mission over nothing but water, the North Sea. I remember up ahead of us but not in our group, there were two ships that ran into each other. I saw a few chutes but I didn't see anything else. That was pretty bad because it was in the wintertime and you couldn't live very long in the cold North Sea water. You had nothing to look forward to if you got out and your chute opened. That was something you thought about when you got back. The guys talked about their reaction of what you would do or not do, but we were pretty low about that. And when you get reports, you don't get the same feeling as when you actually see the result. I didn't see the collision but I saw the chutes, so you know that wasn't something somebody just dreamed up or reported. And there is a difference in actually seeing something and being a part of something like that.

Kiel is a mission that I will always remember, but our last one was Karlsbad. Later, on the map it showed after the war that Russia took it over. It was in a Russian zone and they had another name for it. But at the time it was Karlsbad and why we went down there I have no idea. It was a beautiful mountain town. I forgot why we were even briefed to go down there. What was the reason we were going down there? I forgot what our target was. But we went in and I'll never forget that because it was 12 o'clock noon on a beautiful day and the sun was shining and we had good weather and very little flak, if not at all. I can't remember exactly, but we had probably no opposition and we just unloaded and turned and went back home and that was it. That was the last one.

So I guess that's it for the missions of those that I can remember or the highlights or something that happened on the missions that I'll never forget.

Superstitions, everybody was superstitious. To my knowledge, everyone had these little idiosyncrasies. I remember our radio operator wore his wife's stocking on his head under his helmet. There were guys that carried little booties of their kids, I remember those. And my superstition was my chewing gum, I guess. Another superstition that was pretty common was the way you entered the aircraft. The way you did it the first day you did it from now on just like that. You did it the same way every time. You had the same ritual. I entered through the nose hatch, which is not the easiest way to get in with all the gear. The other pilot, Ed, always entered from the back door and walked all the way through the airplane. That was the little things you did. You didn't want anyone to know that you were superstitious or that you did things like that. Except something like the stocking, that was obvious, you couldn't get around that, you could see it. But I entered the airplane the same way. I also wore the same long underwear and socks the whole time. They were just atrocious. They smelled and everything, but I put them on and I wasn't the only one either. But I wore the same long handle underwear and socks on every mission. I mentioned the gum on the control panel. That was a little superstition. I also had a penny in my shoe, and there is a pretty good story on that. When I was in Tampa, Florida for crew training my bombardier George and I were going to St. Petersburg on Saturday for the weekend. We were dating two girls over there. We were either standing at a bus stop or thumbing a ride and I looked down and I found a penny. I said George, I found a penny and he said put it in your shoe for good luck, so I did. I wore loafers then. So I stuck it in my shoe and not long after that some guy drove up and said "you guys need a ride to St. Pete? I'm going there if you need a ride." So George says, "see John, didn't I tell you!" So things like that you look back and you just say, wow. I carried that penny in my shoe and that penny stayed in my shoe until I was a sophomore or junior in college. I remember the penny, the acid from your foot and everything had worn that thing where you couldn't distinguish Lincoln's picture or anything else. I think to a certain point that we all had some superstitions. You probably picked up a lot, and I wasn't by myself on that either. There were a lot of guys that had superstitions, we just didn't brag about it or let it be known.

I remember one thing that went awry that connects with the superstitions. It might have been that Dresden raid, but anyway, when you get back after debriefing to the Quonset hut, there are other crews in there, the four officers in the crew, and you discuss the mission. There was another pilot who jumped on his copilot, Todd, because things weren't going right. When we put our helmets on, we takeoff our uniform hats, the crushed hats, and put them in a little box behind our seats. Todd had a ground pounding hat on, the one with a grommet in it, and not his crushed hat on this mission. He could have lost his crushed hat, but the pilot just ranted and almost came to blows with Todd because he didn't have his crushed hat. I remember that as far as superstitions were concerned, but you never thought about anything coming to that. They were almost through with their missions and didn't have but a few more left, and they almost came to blows because of the hat. Maybe it was the cognac that they gave us after we got back. If you wanted it, you got a shot of cognac and you took that to debriefing. But all in all we never crossed each other much because your work depended on the other guy. And if it did happen, it was only momentarily and everybody got over it. That's about it for the missions and for the superstitions.

I forget actually the date that we stood down. You would read the Stars and Stripes and we were going so fast, the Russians and us on the ground. But we stood down and there would be no more, and that was a relief. But before that happened, there was one particular thing after it eased up and before we stood down. I remember it was a food drop to the Dutch people. Hitler and the Germans had flooded the country and there were a few high spots. I think Amsterdam was where we dropped the food. But anyway, we were briefed that morning and they took the wooden crates that the bombs came in and loaded them with flour and staples or whatever they could get in there. There was food in the wooden boxes and they somehow strung them up in the bomb bay, like bombs, and we were going to fly over there and drop those wooden boxes full of food in an open space. But we had to get confirmation from the Germans that they were OK with it and they wouldn't shoot at us or anything. Anyway, we were briefed and we went out to the ships and we sat in them and sat there and sat there and finally after a good while they came on and said the Germans never did acknowledge so in that case, the mission that day was scrubbed. We wouldn't go. Just go back to the barracks and see what happens. So we didn't go that day. The next day or two we went up there again, got briefed and this time they had acknowledged. Anyway, we made the mission. It was something to see those people surrounded by water. They had a field and an open space with a white mark on it. We dropped the crates and of course we needed low altitude. We didn't fly like in a bombing run but anyway, that was an experience. I later talked to people that were on the ground at the time. One of them was a little girl about 12 years old and she remembers that it was unique because we hardly ever flew low level stuff. Nobody knew how it was going to work, even those that dreamed it up. But it was a mission that we thought could do some good and it happened and it was really unique.

Later we did another thing that was close to me. We flew to Linz, Austria. They took the airplanes and they floored them with 2 x 4's. They floored in the bomb bay and then they stacked 10-in-1 rations boxes of food. 10-in-1 rations are the things the infantry used. They called it 10-in-1 because 10 men could eat out of one of those boxes. It was a box let's say a foot and a half to two feet long, six or eight inches deep and eight inches wide. It was a nice little container. We were briefed and we went to Linz, which is a long way. Of course, we just flew a skeleton crew which was the pilot, copilot, navigator, and the engineer. There were no gunners, no radio operator, or anything like that. It was a touchy thing because at Linz, we landed at a German fighter base. It had a short runway with buildings all around it. It was a little tricky getting in and getting out of that thing. We knew how to do short field takeoffs and short field landings, but we never had to do that until this time and they went through that with us. We made it and so did the other guys and taxied up and they had somebody to unload the food and stack it beside the airplane. And then they loaded 34 political prisoners or slave laborers or people that had been used by the Germans. I didn't do it, but I think our engineer was probably the one. We sat them throughout the airplane because you had a load factor. We got 34 of them in there and they were emaciated people. They had dysentery and lice. You could tell that they had been through a rough time. We loaded them in there and then came our short field takeoff. In a short field takeoff you take every bit of the runway you can. And you wind up all 4 engines at full throttle while both of the pilots are standing up on the brakes and then you let go and take off. So we were kind of sweating that out, but everybody made a good takeoff and we completed the mission. We flew those people to Orly Field in Paris. We were met by six army trucks and they unloaded the people off the airplane and put them in those trucks and gave each one a little American flag. They were so happy you wouldn't believe it. A couple of guys came around the front of the airplane. We never got out of the cockpit or the flight deck. They couldn't speak English, but they would bow and hold up their fingers on how many years they had been in prison. One of them held up five fingers, he had been in captivity for five years. We had some women in there and I remember their swollen ankles. You could tell that they were malnourished because of the swelling. And anyway, it was just a good feeling to know that you were a part of something like that.

And so what I am saying is that on my tour, a little one, I had a chance to see more than just the killing of people and breaking things. I had a chance to see the other side of it even on the ground in Linz, as we sat there waiting for our people to be brought to us and to be put on the airplane and for the food boxes to be picked up. We were right beside a small road, I guess a country road, but streaming by us within 50 yards or less were all these people with little bundles and little wagons going back home. A lot of those people had to walk all the way back home. I saw that with my own eyes. The refugees and the displaced people and those that lived through it with their little bundles of belongings streaming back to somewhere. And it looks like what you see in the movies. It was a perfect example of all the chaos that was going on after the war, because everybody just quit. There was no leadership, no food, and I'm sure it was hard.

I remember one incident on that mission, there were two little fences that separated us from the road and the refugees and displaced people were streaming by. Every once in a while, somebody would slip through the fences. There were just two or three strands of barbed wire. It was easy to slip under that and come over where we were, and that was where the food boxes were. But I can remember this one guy, you couldn't tell how old he was, but he seemed like an old man. And he slipped under the strand of barbed wire and he made it over and got him a box of food. He had a little bundle, maybe a little sack or something, but he had most everything he owned on him. He looked like he had two or three overcoats on. He got that box, but they had a guard at each place where the food was. He didn't have a gun, he just had a stick. And I'm sure he was under orders not to hurt. Before this there was one guy that slipped under the fence but the guard hit him with a stick and he got back under the wire. But this guy made it and got him a box of food and he was going back and the guard was running behind him and hitting him with that stick. He wasn't hitting him in the head or anything. He was just hitting him on his arms and shoulders so it didn't hurt him because he had so many clothes on. You hoped it didn't hurt him. And he was determined to get that box of food under the fence. He got down and he was going under the wire and the guard never did try to retrieve the food or anything. The guard kept hitting him and finally the old man gave up and went under the fence and left the box of food. And I am thinking, if I could have just hollered and said let that guy alone or something. But that is something I will never forget either. But that is what I remember about that mission to Linz, Austria and the French prisoners, and how happy the people were to get home. We did some good things and that was something that I was a part of and it made me feel good.

Another thing we did in our group was Cook's Tours, and we weren't the only ones that did it. But our ground crew, the cooks, the mechanics, the headquarter guys and all of those that had been a part of the base as long as the war lasted, got to tour some of Germany. If you flew, you flew your missions and when you finished them you got to go home. But these guys had been over here for two or three years and most of them had settled on the base. They were the ones in early '43 that set the base up. But they sweated us out too, especially our mechanics and people that were on the ground. We put them in the airplanes and then went over and showed them just what it looked like. What they were a part of and of course one of the first places that was shown was Cologne. It was absolutely unbelievable. It was just like the pictures you see with the whole city in rubble, crushed bricks and right in the middle of it is a big cathedral standing there with the spire and everything. That was another thing that was pretty good, because there were guys who flew the whole missions and probably never got any lower than 15,000 feet and saw very little of what happened on the ground. Of course, they flew their tour and lived through it and went back home. We got to see what happened on the ground. All the bomb marks, you could see them too. The whole country was torn up. And how they ever put it back together, I don't know. But the Cook's Tours were another thing that was pretty neat that we got to do.

Let's see, VE day was the 8th of May and then we stayed until July probably, actually doing nothing. Waiting to go home. We were packed and you were allowed so much in your B-4 bags and the rest of it was sent in our footlockers by ship, because we were going to fly the airplanes back to the States. So the month of what was left of May and June and part of July was waiting and getting ready and we had to be on alert. There were no leaves, not for the guys that were flying. We took our crew plus 10 other guys. That made 20 people on the airplane. And so you waited until sometime in July and finally an order came down, and we were out of there. We were briefed and we flew to Wales. We landed and fueled up in Wales, and then we were briefed and we took off for Iceland. We landed in Iceland, which was flat with rocks and everything. We never did see darkness because at that time of the year it's daylight all the time. We stayed there maybe a day and the next big briefing was the next leg of a trip home and it was to Greenland, and this was pretty touchy. So during the briefing they briefed us and showed us a movie. They had mounted a camera in the nose of a B-26 and flew that route, with the camera taking pictures, so you knew what you would see, and it was a briefing on how to land in Greenland. We flew to Greenland to a buncher, which was a radio station on the tip of Greenland. Then when you got to that station, you flew in on a beam, hit the corner silence and then you made a turn and went out to the south leg of that beam. And if you were over weather you waited until you broke out and you could see the water down there. And you flew that and you made a procedure turn around and came back to the buncher and to the code of silence and then you flew out the north beam and that put you right up the mouth of the fjord. And you were to hug the left side of the fjord. Don't get over to the right side because there were tributaries we might get mixed up in, and there's no way out of there. But anyway, it was really weird because the next thing was you were flying along and it was almost like flying in a tunnel. There were steep walls on both sides of you. And the next thing was when you see a sunken boat you drop your wheels and 20 degrees flap because the field pops up in front of you. All this time you're looking at a picture of this thing and they're explaining it and sure enough the field just pops up and you are on your approach. You make a slight turn to the right, I think it was, and you're on the approach. Your wheels are down and your flaps are not fully down and you're ready to come in. And sure enough, we had a good day because we broke out and everything went right and it went just like it was shown to us. And coming in on the approach we had a slight tail wind, which was kicking us around, but there was only one way you could land and there was no alternative. You couldn't go around because at the end of the thing was a glacier or a shear wall, and you don't make mistakes. You don't put wheels up and go around because you can't do it. Anyway, at one end of the runway it was on the water, which is zero altitude, and on the other end it was 240 feet. In other words the runway went uphill. Another thing I remember was that we had never landed on a steel mat before. Now the Navy guys, I'm sure in the Pacific and in a lot of places, they were used to such things as steel mats. They built the air strips and they had steel mats and they didn't tell us. It looked just like a regular runway and you couldn't tell it was a steel mat. Anyway, when you hit that steel mat you could imagine the roar of that thing. And you thought, well for crying out loud we've lost the tail wheel and it's come off and something is wrong. Then you realize in a split second that the roar is what you are riding on. Little things like that you're not expecting. I'm sure they've got other things to tell you, instead of saying, OK, you're going to land on a steel mat. But anyway, that was unique in the fact that Greenland, from the air, was absolutely awesome. The icebergs in the water out there before we started up the fjord, were just something to see. We stayed there but I don't remember how long.

And then the next leg home was a long 10-hour hop. We made landfall around Goose Bay, Labrador or Bangor, Maine, I remember that. And then right down New England to Bradley Field, Connecticut. We landed at Bradley Field and got out of the plane and that was the last we saw of that brand new B-17G with all that equipment. We were glad to get back home. And another thing I remember was from there they put us on a train and we went down to Fort Dix, New Jersey and then we went home on leave. I remember riding the train through New York and how the people were hanging out the windows welcoming you home. And the girls with their names and phone numbers on big place cards. It was good to be home. And it wasn't too long after that when we dropped the A-Bomb and that ended that and it was all over for us. It was a good feeling to know you were out of that.

It was quite an experience. It keeps you busy. I was there for almost 2 1/2 years. From June '43 until October '45. That counted training and everything else. But, it was good for us, I guess. I went to school on the G.I. Bill, they educated me. And I had the G.I. Bill on my houses that I bought and the government helped me there.

Zapata: What is one of your fondest memories of the English people?

Ingram: I guess in that area, it was my wash lady, Mrs. D. We called her Mrs. D because her last name started with a D. Mrs.

D's house was right in the base area. She was the wash lady and she took in washing for the guys around the base and you had to more or less be willed a spot on Mrs. D's list because she could only do so many. There were other people doing this for the GIs too. She lived in a little farmhouse. Her husband was a sugar beet farmer and they built the airfield on part of their farm, so he couldn't work. Some of the farmers still raised sugar beets and tilled the field in between the runways. But anyway, he was paid for sacrificing his sugar beet area and Mrs. D took in laundry. We had a ration of soap to do our laundry so we would take our ration up to Mrs. D on our bicycles and give her the soap and our little bundle of clothes and Mrs. D would do our laundry and iron underwear and things. Mrs. D was a talker and most of the time when you got up there she hadn't gotten to yours yet or would be just getting to your bundle. How she did the laundry, I forgot how, but I'm sure it was by hand because there was no such thing as a washing machine. I remember she ironed. They had a big fireplace in the farmhouse. That was the center of the whole house and everything was done at that fireplace. And she cooked. She had a pot of tea going all the time. She had no electricity so she heated the irons on the open fire. And consequently we spent a little time there shooting the breeze with Mrs. D and waiting for our clothes. Mrs. D was very close to all of her guys. She had pictures all over the walls. Oh yeah, they would keep their livestock in the same house. So right next to the kitchen or where the fireplace was, there was a room where they kept the cows. Of course, it was a typical thatched roof house, an East Anglia farmhouse.

Mrs. D was really a character and she had a daughter named Elizabeth. We called her Queen Elizabeth or Princess Elizabeth. She also had a son named Thomas and he was about nine years old I think. Elizabeth was about 12, 13, or 14. She would always hit you up for a picture if you could get one. She had pictures of her guys all over the room where she did the ironing and laundry. She knew the names of those guys, and where they were from and she just talked a steady stream all the time. Mrs. D was really a character and she was one of my favorite English people. We paid her for our laundry and that was her income plus the income from the government for putting airplanes on their sugar beet farm. I will never forget her and neither will any of us. I remember in our group letter years ago when Mrs. D died, they had a big write up about her and I saved it. I think I have it somewhere in my stack of stuff. But there was not a whole lot of interaction with the English people except on leave when you were in London and all of that was a very short thing. You tried to crowd everything into all that you could do. You would meet people on the train going down to London, which is about an hour-and-a-half or maybe a two-hour train trip.

But Mrs. D was the one. That was the highlight of my dealings with the English people. I'll never forget her. She loved it and she loved her part in it. She was taking care of her boys.

End.

Audio version of the interview in the Library of Congress: https://www.loc.gov/item/afc2001001.34401/

John's Letters

LETTERS

These are the actual letters he wrote home. They describe his journey and life in the Eighth Air Force. They are transcribed in their original form.

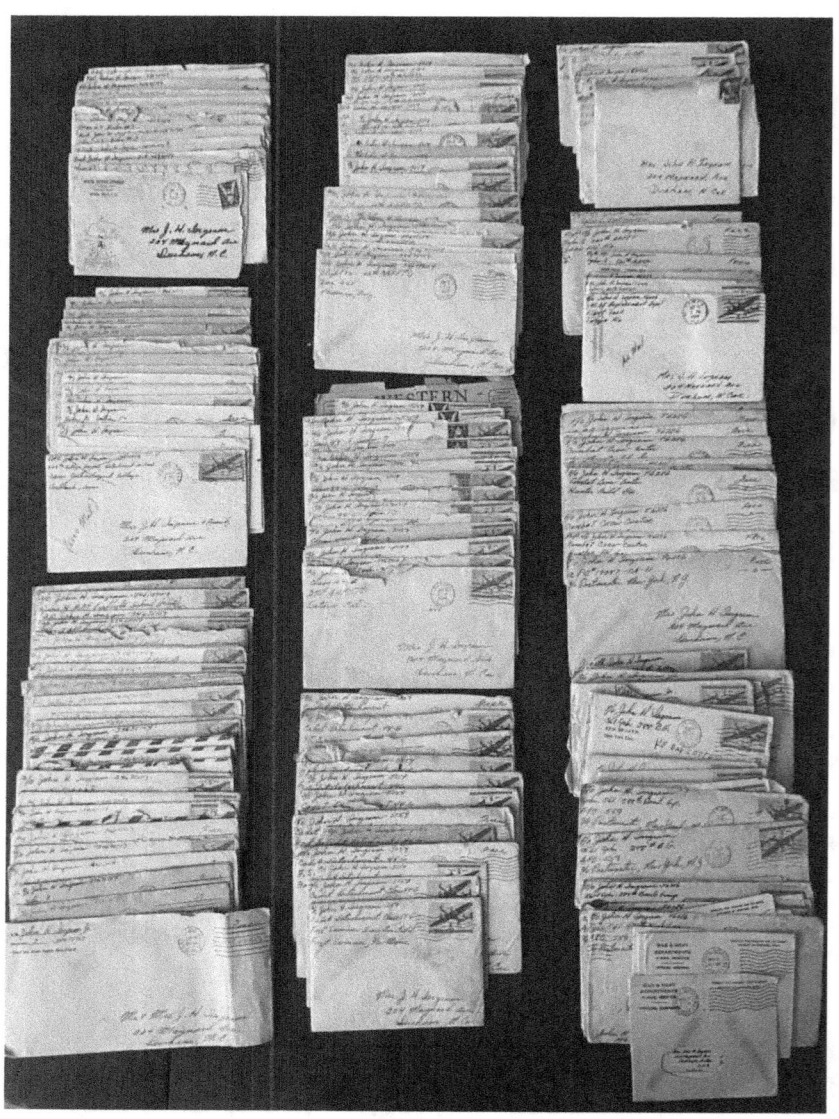

This is a list of people that John mentions in his letters. They are his family, girlfriends, and friends from back home

Family:
LaMarr-brother (4 years old when John left home for the Army Air Corps)
Evelyn-sister (16 years old when John left home for the Army Air Corps)
Ingram/Neathery-his Dad's side of the family
Uncle Henry-his Dad's brother
Uncle Edgar-his Dad's brother
Aunt Beatrice - his Dad's sister
Mildred-his Mom's niece
Aunt Ethel - his Mom's sister
Uncle Harry - Aunt Ethel's husband
H.G- cousin, Aunt Ethel's and Uncle Harry's son, in the Marines
Uncle Eddie - his mother's brother

Girlfriends:
Deedee - high school classmate
Charlotte - high school classmate
Wanda - high school classmate
Blonde Bomber - high school classmate
Patty - girlfriend in Tampa
Shooks - girlfriend at Texas Tech
Julie - girlfriend in Phoenix

Friends and Teachers back in North Carolina (NC):
Warren Pendergraph - high school classmate (best man in his wedding)
Sam Hughs - high school friend
Mr. Stutts - friend of family
Miss Hobgood - high school teacher
Miss Boland - high school teacher
Hall Miles - high school classmate
Gorden Whitted - high school classmate
Caroline Lockhart - high school friend
Carlyle Council - high school friend

James Wallers -friend
Mac McCullen - high school friend
Mrs. Ezell - family friend
Jimmy Knight - brother of Mrs. Ezzle
Ma Gholson - high school teacher
Tommy Fowler - high school classmate
Ed Monk - high school friend
Jr Henson - friend
Betty Jean Price - high school classmate
Bobby Eblen - friend
Steve Killenbrew - friend
Thomas Jones - high school friend
Holton - high school friend
Scotty - friend
Mutt - high school friend
Rudy - friend
Specio - high school friend
Totsy - friend
Judson Pickert - high school classmate
Betty Peak - family friend
Bill Haire -friend
Ham - friend
Hildo - friend
Cotton - friend from Durham, NC
H.D Leigh - friend

June 4 - July 24, 1943

Ft. Bragg, NC
and
Keesler Field, MS

At Crescent Beach, South Carolina with his high school friends before he has to report to Keesler Field, Mississippi

Photos of Keesler Field Basic Training Center in his annual from the base

INTERIOR OF BARRACK   BARRACK FOR ENLISTED MEN
BACHELOR OFFICERS' QUARTERS

Photos of Keesler Field Basic Training Center in his annual from the base

TENT AREA

For the men who spend their spare time at camp, the squadron day
rooms are favorite hangouts. This group has just received its copies of
The Keesler Field News, the Field's weekly publication.

HOSTESS HOUSE   FIELD POST OFFICE

*Photos of Keesler Field Basic Training Center in his annual from
the base*

June 6, 1943
Crescent Beach, South Carolina
Sunday

Dear Mom,

Well we finally got down here. I thought we were going to be in Fort Bragg the rest of our lives. I took the oath about 5 PM, Friday evening, and left Fayetteville about 7 PM. We made it to Florence, South Carolina that night, stayed over and got in here about noon yesterday.

Everyone is having a swell time. The bunch here is leaving either Tuesday or Wednesday, and we have a free ride home. So I guess we will see you Tuesday or Wednesday. I don't know when I will be called, but I expect it will be soon. If you do hear anything, you can reach me at: Ocean Strand Hotel, Crescent Beach, South Carolina. (phone: 9152)

Well I think I'll turn in now. You all take good care of grandmother, and I will see you soon. Don't worry about me.

Love, Private J.H. Army Enlisted Reserve

June 24,1943
Air Corps Technical School, Keesler Field, Mississippi
Thursday, PM

    Dear Mom and Dad,

    I haven't had time to think so far. They keep us so busy here, but it's raining now and we are off for a while. The train ride down here wasn't so bad, in fact it was the shortest ride I ever took. We got here about 7:30, Tuesday morning, and they've kept us on the go ever since. I've got more clothes now than I thought I'd ever have. I have everything now but my shots, and I guess it won't be long until we get those.

    The boys are alright, and us rebels stick together. We get up at 5 o'clock AM every morning, and I nearly starve before chow time. The days seem like weeks. It was pretty lonesome the first few days, but now we are pretty well organized and things are livening up a bit. We are treated well here.

    They call us specialists. This is an Air Corps Technical Center, and there are only a few of us cadets here. This is where we get our basic training, military discipline, marching, and physical fitness. We will only be here for 28 days at the most. By the way, I just took out $10,000 in insurance, and you and dad are the beneficiaries. After our 28 days are over, we will go to college, and that is what I am looking forward to. I sure would like to be home, but this is it and with your helping prayers, I am going to make this great. Our officers and non-coms are very nice, and they don't kick you around like they say they do.

Well, there's that bugle again, and we will have to fall out, so that is all for this time, but I will write you tomorrow. Tell everyone to write to me and kiss Lamar for me. Bye bye and may God bless you.

Love, Son

(I'm sending you a book to give you an idea of what this place looks like.)

June 26,1943
Air Corps Technical School, Keesler Field, Mississippi
Saturday PM

Hello Mom and Dad,

Just a word before the lights go out to let you know that I am still kicking. The training is getting tougher and tougher as the days go by. We all gripe about it, but stick to it just the same. This business of writing is really a problem. We get up at 5 AM, which just gives you time to eat and take a crap. Then we are on the ball from then to 7 PM, and after days like that you can hardly pick up a pen. Besides, we have to do all our washing and cleaning at night. So if you don't hear from me too often, it's not because I don't want to write. I think I can get in at least 3 or 4 letters a week.

I hope you will enjoy the book I sent you, and when I get down to the main px again, I'll see if I can pick up anything else to send you. I took a physical exam today, and I am due for my shots Monday. The only thing I dread though is when they start working on my teeth. By the way, I've gained 2 pounds these 5 days I've been here, and it would suit me fine if I keep that up. I went into town this morning on mail detail. The little bay is right on the gulf, and there are some beautiful hotels on the bay drive. The 59th is shipping out Monday, and we are next in line to leave this place. So if we are lucky we may not be here the full 28 days.

Well, I've got 10 minutes until lights go out, and I've got 2 pairs of fatigues and a pair of socks to wash out. So be good and write me, all of you. Good night.

Love, Son

(Mom there are a few things I want you to send me. My red swimming trunks, my white swimming trunks, jockey, my shoes, and rationing tickets. How about buying me a good harmonica at one of the pawn shops. And send me one in the key of G. Thats all I can think of now. If I do think of anything else, I will let you know. Oh yes, grandmother and grandad's address. And anybody else you can think of. Tell everyone to write me.)

June 28, 1943
Air Corps Technical School, Keesler Field, Mississippi
Monday AM

Hello Folks,

I have a few minutes at ease, so I'll let you know I'm still kicking. Yesterday I took the classification test, which consists of one aeronautical classification, and the regular army classification test. I don't know about the first test, but on the second test I qualified for officers training school incase I wash out of the cadets. In other words, if I wash out of the cadets, I'm qualified to become an officer in whatever branch I select.

The training is getting tougher everyday. And we run on a 7 day schedule. We get a couple of hours off on Sunday morning for church. Hall Miles, and Gordon Whitted, all that bunch from Durhum, got in here yesterday, and I was sure glad to see them. For a while I thought I was going to be the only Tar Heel here. They are in the 606 squadron. I'm having a big time here now. I lead the singing in our squadron. We sing while we march, which kind of makes the drilling more fun. You never know what you're going to do next around here. So I can only tell you what I've done.

Mom, see if you can arrange it so I can get the morning paper down here. I'd like to keep up with the things at home.

Well there's chow call, and I'll have to stop now. I'll write you every chance I get. Tell everyone hello and write me. Be good and keep your fingers crossed for me.

Love, Son (Don't forget to send me those things I told you about.)

June 30, 1943
Air Corps Technical School, Keesler Field, Mississippi
Wednesday PM

Hello Folks,

I just received your letters and it put me right on top of the water tank, which is the highest thing around here. We're still working like dogs. Camp Butner was never like this. We are always on the alert to ship out of here. So they are trying to jam and pack all the training they can get into us, so we will be ready for college. Our squadron was on KP today. They got us up at 2:15 this morning. It's 7:30 PM now. I got to sit down for about 45 minutes this morning. We got our rifles this evening and we are going to the field with them tomorrow with full equipment. So I'm going to have to turn in early tonight.

Hall Miles and the boys said to tell everyone hello. Gordon Whitted has been in the hospital everyday since he's been here. And if he doesn't hurry up and get out, I'm afraid he won't be able to make it. One boy in our barracks was the same way and he's home now. I tried to write everybody I know, but I have such little time to do it in. Send me any mail I get and also Mutt's and the boys addresses. I sure was shocked about Rudy's mother. I bet he took it kind of hard. You be careful ya here! haha

Mom, I could write you a book if I just had time. But if I don't get to bed I might not make it tomorrow. Tell Evelyn and everyone to write me. I'm working my head off and I got my heart and soul in this thing for y'all and for my good too, so keep rooting for me and praying for me, because I'll never do it unless you are behind me. You may think and I may think that I'm out on my own now, and it's up to me, but I can see now that I still need your coaching, and backing if I am to make the grade. Write to me and tell everybody you see to do the same.

Well, I'll have to close now and catch that dream train home. That's what we call hitting the hay. It pulls out of here at 9 o'clock for all points of the country.

Good night and Keep Me Flying!

Love, Son

July 2, 1943
Air Corps Technical School, Keesler Field, Mississippi
Friday PM

Hello Mom and Folks,

By the way, your letter said you haven't received but one letter. Well I've got three more as I know of in the mail right now. I don't know why you haven't gotten them. I guess it does take a lot of time since there's so much mail going out of here and coming in. I was glad to hear from Evelyn. Tell Dad and LaMarr to write to me. I hope I can last through this.

I got some more shots today, and my arm is about to drop off. The training is getting tougher and more interesting everyday. We're drilling with and learning how to handle the M1 Garand rifles now. We will probably hit the firing range and gas chamber next week, also we have to run the bayonet course in 40 seconds. This training is to toughen us up, and teach us military discipline, and it's doing a good job of it.

I have to stop a minute, the boys are rolling in the floor laughing at my haircut. I just went over and got my head almost shaved. We really got a good bunch of boys except a few guys that are right sneaky. They call me Tarheel and Johnny. I keep them laughing all the time with my southern drawl and slang. Most of them are from Pennsylvania and up north.

I've noticed Whitted and the rest came in with the southern bunch. Gordon is out of the hospital. I saw Thomas Jones today and he heard from his brother, who was with Mutt and the gang. They're only ten miles away from here over at Gulfport field going through their basic training too. I've heard from Specio, Caroline Lockhart, and one or two more, but I still haven't heard from Warren. You tell him he better write me.

We are taking an Aircraft Recognition Course, we are learning to recognize all enemy planes as well as our own. At one hundredth of a second, that is, they flash a picture on the screen at one hundredth of a second and we have to name it, tell how many there were, and give the distinctive features of the plane. Man, you really have to be on the ball.

It has rained down here for the last five days, but we don't let that stop us, and it's all I can do to keep my clothes dry so I won't catch pneumonia. Well I better close for tonight. The party is getting rough up here. I stay on the second floor of the barracks. Tell everyone hello and write to me everyday if you can. Good night all.

Love, Son

Give everybody my address and send me James Wallers, so I can look him up. Don't forget to send me those things I told you. **Keep me Flying!**

July 3, 1943
Air Corps Technical School, Keesler Field, Mississippi

Hello Folks,

Just a line before I turn in. Tomorrow is our first day off since we've been here and I sure can use it. They haven't slacked up on us at all. We are still going full blast from 5 AM to 7 PM. We're scheduled for the rifle range next week and I'm looking forward to that. We are learning to use the Thomson Automatic 45 caliber and the 03.

I didn't feel so good today, I had some more shots yesterday and my arm was sore today. I will take a good laxative tonight. I think maybe it will do the trick.

I've heard from quite a few people, but nothing does me any better than a letter from home. I hope I get the other letters soon because I sure could use some hangers, my harmonica, and swimming trunks. All of us boys are planning on going swimming down in the Gulf tomorrow.

Well I guess that's about all I know tonight. Keep writing and write more often. Tell everyone hello. I'll write you again Monday night.

Love, Son

July 5,1943
Air Corps Technical School, Keesler Field, Mississippi
Monday PM

Hello Folks,

Man, I hit jackpot today! I got 2 letters and the package from you today. I sure was glad to hear from you. Keep it up! The harmonica is alright. The boys went crazy over my playing. The trunks are alright too. We had the day off yesterday and we all went swimming down in Back Bay. The whole camp was there I think. The boats and fishing tackle were all free.

We had it easy today too. I think I worked about 1 hour and 15 min the whole day, but I guess they will make up for it tomorrow. They are getting strict on us now. They figure we are supposed to know right from wrong and for now it's "on the ball" or guard duty. There are all kinds of rumors about when we ship out, but we never can get anything definite.

Tell everyone hello and write me. I'll try to write you everyday.

Love, Son (Send me some more addresses)

July 7,1943
Air Corps Technical School, Keesler Field, Mississippi
Wednesday PM

Hello Folks,

Well I made it to today, and each day is getting tougher. I'm giving it all I got though. James Wallers came up to see me tonight. Someone sent him my address. He didn't shoot me any bull like I expected. He is in Aircraft Mechanic School and is expecting to finish up pretty soon. From here, he doesn't know where he'll go. I'll see him again tomorrow night and I will tell you all about it. One fellow in our barracks already has his shipping orders. So I guess I can look forward to about 10 more days here.

I didn't get a letter today and I don't feel like I lived today. In the army you don't think for yourself, so the only time I feel like I am really living is when I hear from home.

I got to go now Mom, the lights are out and the mosquitoes are about to eat me up. So write to me and send me anything and everything you can. Don't hold back. Tell everyone hello.

Goodnight All, Son

July 10,1943
Air Corps Technical School, Keesler Field, Mississippi
Saturday AM

Hello Folks,

I just got back from the drill field. We had a review this morning for some big General. My back is about to break. We stood at attention for 2 solid hours with the sweat running down your eyes and you couldn't even lift a finger. Our squadron won the ribbon for matching and singing. The reserve men in our squadron are on alert now and I will probably ship out tomorrow, which means they say that we will be gone by next weekend. I hope so anyway.

There are all kinds of rumors about where we go, but nothing is definite. The fifty ninth, which shipped the day before yesterday, is at North Carolina State College in Raleigh. I sure would like to be that lucky. I did KP again yesterday from 2:15 AM till 7:30 PM, about 16 or 18 hours straight.

Mom, I got my mail alright. I got the package too and don't forget to send me anything you want and can. I guess that's about all right now. I'll write you Monday. Tell everyone hello and to keep writing. I'll call you when we get our shipping orders, I hope it will be next weekend. Bye bye and be sweet.

Love, Son

July 11, 1943
Air Corps Technical School, Keesler Field, Mississippi
Sunday PM

Hello Folks,

Well there's not that much news today. We had the day off and I've had my pants on once today to go to chow. I've really been taking it easy. All of our spirits are high tonight. We are on the alert to move out at any time now. It may be Thursday and it may be two or three weeks, but it still gives you a good feeling to know what is in front of you.

We received field packs and I guess that means we have a tough week ahead. I get a lot of mail every now and then, but I could never get enough. Warren hasn't written to me yet, you tell him he better write. Charlotte writes to me everyday, can you imagine that. Don't worry, I'm taking every precaution with that.

I heard from Aunt Ethel. She said she hasn't heard from H.G. yet. I don't know much more to tell you except that I love you all, and I'd give anything to get home just for a few minutes. Believe me when my time is up in this man's army, I'm coming right home and sit down on my can till the roof falls on top of me.

Tell everyone hello and write to me. Please send me anything you want to. If I ever get time I'll send you all something to remember me by.

Love, Son

July 13, 1943
Air Corps Technical School, Keesler Field, Mississippi

Hello Folks

I got 3 letters from you today. Thank you for the good luck piece. I hope it does bring me luck, I need it.

Well I'm a tired soldier tonight. We had a heck of a hard day today and KP is coming up again tomorrow. We get KP about twice a week now. We had a good little hike today, with full pack. I sure will be glad when we do a little riding, if anything like that is possible.

I heard from Warren today for the first time. He seems to be having a good time. He didn't mention work. I wrote to grandmother and grandad, but I haven't heard from them yet. It's kind of hard to write now, at first everything was new to me and I could write plenty, but now it's the same old thing everyday and there's not that much news to tell you. I've been getting the paper pretty good, but something has happened to it these past few days.

I sure do hope I can get closer to home, so it won't take my mail so long to get to me. Well that is about all I know that's good. Things don't happen as fast here as they do back home. Keep writing, and how about sending me some of that air corps stationary.

Hug and kiss everyone for me and tell them all I will be home Christmas if I have to go awol. Good night, and keep those home fires burning.

Love, Son

(Don't worry about that Yankee Brogue. It's going to take more than an army to change me. I'm still the same, and always will be)

July 14, 1943
Air Corps Technical School, Keesler Field, Mississippi
Wednesday, PM

Hello Folks,

Well there goes another day and it's time to think about home now. We had it tough again today out on the rifle range. We haven't tried for score yet, we were just practicing the care and cleaning of a rifle and how to aim and fire it. The shipping days are getting closer now, and I sure will be glad to get out of these gates. By the way, we have gas drill tomorrow. Here's hoping my gas mask doesn't leak.

I looked for my package today, I sure would like to get anything you all would like to send. I got three newspapers today, they even come in bunches. They really make me feel at home. I heard from grandmother today, she says that Uncle Henry and Uncle Edgar are going to write me.

Mom, that's about all the good news I know. I got a lot of washing to do tonight and I dread it. The darn things are so hard to get clean. Good night Mom. Keep thinking about me and writing me. I'm working awful hard for this, and If I make it I'll be the proudest boy in town.

By the way Mom, send me a fountain pen. I can't buy one here and I have to borrow one every time I write. Also my ring, if it's fixed. Goodnight all.

Love, Son

July 20,1943
Air Corps Technical School, Keesler Field, Mississippi
Tuesday PM

Hello Everybody,

Well I guess you all wonder why you haven't heard anything from me for the past few days. Well here's how it is. I wanted to surprise you by sending you a telegram from some college, but it looks like I'll have to spill the beans. We went on the alert last Sunday and we're scheduled to be shipped out of here tomorrow, which is Wednesday. We got everything ready to go, had our physical and everything. Then the whole works blew up in our faces, just like everything else here does. About an hour ago they told us that our transportation had been messed up and our shipping orders had been canceled, indefinitely. But we are still on the alert and may leave any minute.

About half of the boys left this morning and I sure do miss them. We all hated to see them go. We made such close friendships between us, but I guess that's another thing I will have to get used to.

I told you about them getting my pay messed up. Well I finally got it straightened out and I was payed off for the first time today. I drew $16.67 today and signed the payroll for next month.

Well Mom, that's about all the news here right now. Oh! By the way, I got my package, and all the fruit was spoiled. So don't send any more fruit..

It sure is a relief to finish up with this basic training. We really had it tough, but that part is all over now and we are taking it easy for a change. And I have to go now, but I'll let you know if anything comes up. Keep rooting for me, because right now this means more to me than anything I know of and I have got to make good, not only for myself, but for you and Dad.

Goodnight all, and love from your Son

July 24, 1943
Air Corps Technical School, Keesler Field, Mississippi
Saturday

Hello Folks,

It just came over the PA System. We will ship out tomorrow morning for I don't know where. I haven't got time to tell you much more but I will write you the very first minute I get there. I just hope and pray they will send us somewhere near home.

Tell Aunt Ethel that I have written HG twice and I haven't heard from him yet. I hope Evelyn likes her kerchief. I will send you something next. It's goodbye to Keesler Field. Bye bye and stick with me Mom and Dad, this is my one and only break of my life and I gotta make good for both of you.

Believe it or not, it was 118 degrees here today and over 300 hundred soldiers passed out today on the drill field. Now you see why I want to get out of this place. Goodbye and God keep you till I get home again.

Love, Son

JULY 28 - SEPTEMBER 27, 1943

LUBBOCK, TX

"A picture of the flight boys right before we left for the field"

"This is me and my roommates getting ready for Saturday inspection. The two in the rear are from South Carolina and Raleigh, North Carolina. The one seated up front is from Cincinnati, Ohio. I am in the back right. This Texas sun has put a good tan on me."

Picture of classes at Texas Tech in his annual from the base

Picture of Texas Tech in his annual from the base

Squadron G — Flight 54
John H. Ingram Jr.
204 Maynard Ave
Durham, NC

Wednesday, July 28, 1943

Hello folks,

My hunch was right, we are here in Lubbock Texas, at Texas Tech and is it a swell place except I can't help but think how far I am from home. We left Keesler Sunday morning, 500 of us by troop train and arrived here Tuesday. This is a nice college but for the first 21 days we aren't allowed to see much of this place. In just plain words, it's heaven compared to Keesler. The food is better than any I've ever tasted. We live in a new brick dormitory, four men to a room. Our classes consist of physics, math, english, geography, and history and they are a long way from being anything like high school courses.

Lubbock is a clean modern little town of about 40,000 people and I've never seen the likes of so many good looking girls. It's in the north western part of Texas near Amarillo, look it up on the map.

We are supposed to get nine months of academic courses here crammed into five months and we will also do a little flying here too. When we were moved from Keesler, we were changed from the fourth service command to the ninth west coast command which means that I will go to Santa Ana California for classification next and there's not much of a chance of me seeing you all for a very long time. I'm getting kinda used to it now though. I am really seeing a lot of this country and it's really worth fighting for. When this war is over, I'd like for us to take a real trip and let me show you just what I've seen and will see.

I'll be here for at least three or four months, so don't hesitate about sending me my ring, pen, stationary, or anything else. You will hear from me only about two or three times a week now because I have to do too much studying, but write to me as often as you can.

If I stay on the ball and work hard I'll make the grade. You could never realize just what you have to do and go through to be a pilot. You have to be almost perfect in every respect, but if you all will stick with me I won't worry about a thing.

I gotta go now but I'll write more when I get a chance.

Lots of love,

Son

Saturday, July 31, 1943

Hello folks,

I'm all settled now and we started today digging into those books. We had two classes of physics, math, english, and history and they go so fast with it that you have to stay on the ball to grasp it. Our professors are good and I think I'll get along with them swell, at least I hope so.

We are still confined to the post except for an hour a day they let us go across the street to the drugstores. In about two weeks though, we will get the weekends off and I'm sure looking forward to it. It's been almost 7 weeks now since I walked down a city street free to do what I want to. I have a swell bunch of roommates, three of us rebels against one yank but we will get along fine together.

So far as comfort is concerned this is just like the Washington Duke hotel. The food is better than what I got at home. (Not throwing you off on your cooking mom), except I miss your good little biscuits.

We had to make a short talk in english class this morning about our past life and our post war plans and they all died laughing when I said, when this war is over, I was going home and sit down.

The grind is getting tougher and tougher and I see that I am in for some hard work that can be realized only by an air cadet, but you all keep praying for me, I'm doing my best. If I wash out I don't believe I would want to come home for a long time, but I'm not.

I got too close now, send me anything you think I would need.

Love, Son

God bless you all, and me too!

(If you can send these, I would appreciate it. Tennis racket and anything you can get in the way of athletic clothes. See if I have got some basketball shoes, shorts, and sweat clothes around the house. I would love to have the badminton set if you don't use it anymore)

Saturday, August 1943

Hello folks,

It's me again and tired as usual. I just got paid, I drew $37 and right now it doesn't seem worth it but they tell us we are not in the army for the money. I was just thinking of this time last year when I was drawing around $125 a month.

They worked us so hard yesterday. We didn't get a chance to study last night and I had a physics test and an english test this morning, but I think I did pretty good on them. My average in math is 98.

We had a little pep talk last night from our new CEO and it really put the life in us. They seem like they are so sure we will make the grade and they actually have us believing it.

Flight 51 starts flying Monday. I am in 54 so I guess it will be just a matter of a few weeks before we will start flying. I don't like that because I wanted to get all the studying I could in. You see we drop our courses when we start flying. When we go to Santa Ana they give you stiff exams and I want to be well prepared for it, but I guess I'll have to pray as usual that I will pass and do the best I can.

I don't know what I'm going to do if I don't get some mail. Please write to me as often as you can. Tell Dad to write too. I'd like to hear from him again.

They haven't let us out yet, but I'll think about next weekend, if we stay on the ball, we will get open post. From what I have seen in the stores across the street, I think I can find a lot of gadgets you would like to have. Don't tell LaMarr, but I am having a nice little pair of real cowboy boots made up for him with all the trimmings. I hope he can stand up in those high heels.

I've got two of my uniforms draped up yesterday. I had the shirt cut down in the waist so it would fit me close and my pants were a little too long so I had them taken up. They sure do soak us down here for cleaning and just about everything else. The merchants should realize that we only get $37 a month and most of the time we don't get that.

I had a letter from Uncle Edgar the other day and he said he's up for a promotion soon. I wrote to him all about my army life too.

Well, that's about all I know right now so I better close now and get my shoes shined and fall out for retreat but I'll write again soon. In the meantime, write me a book, ha ha. You need not send a badminton set, we have one now.

Love,

Son

Wednesday, August 4, 1943

Hello folks,

I'm looking for a letter from you any day now. It's been about two weeks now since I heard from you last. I just got off of guard duty. I've been on it since 6 PM yesterday and my back is about to break. I missed all my classes today on that account and I got a lot of work to do to catch up. Our week is really hard and every little minute is taking up. We have classes from 8 AM to 3 PM and then from 3 PM to 5 PM we have physical training and drills.

Just as soon as I get kind of adjusted to the schedule I'll like it fine. Only about one more week and we will begin to get the weekends off. I am already for it too. The photographers have been taking pictures around here all week for a book of our unit. It's just like my high school Messenger except that it's about our college days in the Air Corps. I had my individual picture taken for it today. I hope it comes out good. I'm sending you the book when it is finished. See if you can spot me in the formation and in the physical training drill. (Class room also)

Well, I gotta close now and get in them books. Write to me every hour and don't forget, I got to make this! Don't worry about me, I can!

Love,

Son

Friday, August 6, 1943

Hello Folks,

I just got a minute or two between now and the next class, so I'll drop you a line while I'm waiting. Well, I didn't get any mail again today and it looks like everybody has forgotten about me or else I'm so far out in the sticks they must send it by pony express. I hope I will hear from you soon.

This college business is sure about to get me down. We stay on the go from 6 AM to 8:30 PM and the other hour and five minutes I'm in those books. They say you gain weight in the army but I guess they really mean the army, not the air corps. We don't even get time to rest our weary bones. Sometimes I get fed up with all this stuff but I get over it. If they would just let us out of this place once in a while it wouldn't be so bad.

Well I have to fall out now and I'll write again soon. You all be good and stay with me, I need it.

See ya,

Love,

Son

Thursday, August 12, 1943

Hello folks,

I got your letter today and was sure glad to hear from you. Evelyn tickled me telling me about her boyfriend. I know the boy, at least I had seen him over at the pool and he seemed to be a pretty nice fellow.

Well, I got good news for you. We get our first open post this weekend from Saturday evening till Sunday night and I can hardly wait for them to turn us loose. Man, it's really going to feel good to have a few hours to do what you please. I'll have my picture made and send it to you.

It's still the same old place here but they get tougher every day. All of our officers graduated from West Point and they run this place just like West Point. Everything we do we do at attention, we even have to eat at attention with one hand in our lap. I get letters from some of my buddies who were shipped to other places and it makes me sick. They have open post every night and weekend, they don't have to wear ties on the campus and all the stuff we get here. I keep telling myself that it's better that they be that way here. I can't help but to think that I'm just unlucky. This West Coast command is really tougher than the east and they wash more out like nobody's business. I'll make it though.

Well I got a quit now and get in the books because grades go in this Saturday. Take it easy and stick with me, cause I've been through too much already to drop out.

Love,
Son

Sunday

Hello folks,

It's me and I'm just about all in after two days of open post. We were turn loose yesterday evening and it was just like a stampede, they were running in all directions. Five of us went to town and spent about 2 1/2 hours running in and out of the stores. About 9:30 we got up a bunch and went out to the Cotton Club. This club is a nice place, something like a nightclub with a floor show and everything. The orchestra was good and we had a good time dancing. Bill Haire, from Winston Salem, and I got started with that N.C. Jitterbug and they wouldn't let us stop the whole time we were there. We didn't do much today, played tennis most of the day and sat in the drugstore the rest. By the way, I got your package yesterday and was tickled pink. Everything is fine and dandy.

Yesterday morning ended our first report period, I guess you would call it. Grades went in Saturday evening and I think I came out pretty good. I had a 84 average in physics, 98 average in math, 100 average in geography, and about 75 or 80 average in English, and we didn't get a grade in history this time. I hope I can hold that.

I like it a lot better now since you can kind of look forward to the weekends off. I better close now, I got guard duty all night and tomorrow and I better catch a couple hours sleep before I go on. You all take it easy and keep your fingers crossed for me and I'll write again soon. Goodnight.

Love,
Son

Wednesday

Hello Folks,

Well I hit the jackpot yesterday, I got a whole bunch of letters from Keesler field. Some of them had been there for almost a month. I also got about a month's supply of newspapers. The paper is coming here pretty regularly now and I really do look forward to that almost as much as I do for a letter from home.

I still got my nose to the grind, I worked on a long physics problem today and the whole class liked to have fainted. Next week I'll be an upperclassman. I've been taking a lot of riding from the upperclassman but now it's my turn and I am going to dish it out.

I got a proof of my picture they took for the annual and it turned out pretty good. I've ordered a 5 x 7 enlargement of it and I will send it to you as soon as I get it. It's really not bad, I think I look fat as a butterball.

By the way, since you asked about it, I'm no longer a private, I'm an a/s Aviation student. Sounds good doesn't it! That's just another step toward being appointed an aviation cadet and if I get that nothing will stop me. You see when we go to Santa Ana for 48 days of classification we go through the stiffest mental and physical exams and if you pass you go on from there. The boys tell me not to worry about it since I took a number 64 exam at Goldsboro. They say if you can pass that you have a good chance at Santa Ana. I won't worry because I know that there are so many people depending on me and I've just got to make it.

Keep praying for me and I'll give it all I got. Tell everybody hello and I'll write again soon.

Love,

Son

Monday

Hello Mom,

I'm on sick call today, went out and had my teeth worked on. I'm going back tomorrow for a filling and gum treatment. The doc is a nice guy and he does good work. You have to be almost dead before you can go on sick call here. I hope I won't miss much in my classes but after all, this is more important than the schooling.

I had a grand weekend. I really enjoy these weekends and it kinda gives you something to look forward to. A bunch of us went to the Fair Saturday night and took in everything.

I missed my church this Sunday, nobody woke me up Sunday morning and I slept right through it. I try to go every Sunday. I have been going to church right here on the post. The minister and pianist come out and we have open air service every Sunday morning but this Sunday they didn't come. I like him a lot because he reminds me of Reverend Yates.

Three of us ran into some nice girls Sunday evening. They had a car and of course we had a grand time. We toured the city and ended up out at McKinney Park on a picnic. It reminded me so much of our old gang at home.

Well there's a rumor in the air that we will start flying next Monday. I don't know how true it is but right now everything points in that direction.

We are having retreat now and you should see it. It's very formal with the band and everything. We have a large crowd of the town folks out every evening to see it, and we really strut our stuff for that. Ask dad, he knows all about what happens at retreat.

Evelyn has written to me from Dansville twice and I enjoy her letters so much. I guess she'll be grown up and married before I see her again. LaMarr is the one I'd like to see. The way you talk he is really shooting up.

The boys are coming in off the drill field now and in a few minutes they will be falling out for retreat. I hate sick call, you miss everything that goes on.

I get all your letters and packages and you can't imagine how much I enjoy them. I never worry about mail cause I know there will always be one from home.

I know dad is catching it tough with no help and I sure wish I was there to help him.

I better close now and get dressed for chow . I'll keep writing as often as I can. You take it easy and don't worry about me because I am sure well taken care of and as far as comfort goes, I am as much at ease as I've ever been and I am in love with this cadet training.

Goodbye and I love you all,

J.H.

Wednesday

Hello folks,

I have a few spare minutes to give you the latest at Texas Tech.

I went back to the coal miner (dentist) yesterday and he gave me a gum treatment. He also gave me some mouthwash to use three times a day. I'm going back again tomorrow and get them cleaned.

We took our flight physical yesterday and we start flying Monday. This is our last week of academic work and in a way I am glad of it, yeh! We were supposed to be here five months but the way it looks now we will be out of here by the middle of next month. I believe they are rushing us through a little too fast.

I got the little bird and all the other packages. You don't know how much I like to get packages. The bird is really going to be my good luck charm and it's going up with me every time.

I better stop now and get ready for my next class. Keep writing and I love you all. Tell Evelyn to keep writing too.

Love, Son

Tell dad to write when he can.

Wednesday

Hello folks,

Yep, I'm a hot pilot now and I love it. So far I've got three whole hours in my little logbook and they are like a dream to me. The first day it was pretty rough up there but since then it's been nice and I really learned a lot. We go out again tomorrow morning and my instructor told me today that tomorrow we would get in a few stalls and spins. Here's where I find out whether my stomach will hold out or not. Yesterday he gave me the stick and I climbed to 2000 feet, made a 90° turn to the left and a 45° turn to the right, went into a gentle glide, pulled out and leveled off and honestly folks I felt like rearing back in that seat and singing at the top of my voice. It really gives you a good feeling to make that plane do what you want it to do. When we came down, he said I slipped a little in my turn, due to too much rudder, but he said I would soon get the feel of it and make them without slipping. I wish I could get you a picture of me in all the flying equipment, chute, glasses and everything. I really look like a flier whether I am or not. They won't let us take any pictures out there so I guess you'll just have to wait for a picture of me later. Well I could just go on like this all night when it comes to the business of flying but I guess it bores you a little.

I thought about Evelyn starting back to school today. What teachers has she got and what kind of courses is she taking? I see by the paper that football practice has started and it looks like the draft has hit the team pretty hard.

Tell LaMarr I may be a little late with his birthday package but I haven't forgotten him. Last week my money was pretty low but I got paid yesterday and you tell him that he can expect a package sometime next week. I sure would like to see him.

Well, I better wind up this thing now and get to work on my flight notebook. We have to keep notes of everything we do and learn. They'll probably grade them tomorrow and I have to get mine up to date.

Tell dad to take it easy and you all keep praying for me because I got to make it. Good night and I love you all.

Son, Capt. Johnny Ingram U.S.A.A.F.

Friday

Hello folks,

I started this letter last night but all I got written was Friday. The lieutenant called us all out and took eight of us with type O blood out to the S.P.A.A.F. Base for an emergency transfusion. They took four of the boys and they said if they needed another transfusion the other four of us would be called.

I am getting along rather good in my flying, we have been up every day this past week except Wednesday. We leave for the field today in about two hours. The way the weather looks now, it's going to be pretty rough up there today. The hotter it is, the rougher it will be due to hot air rising. I did a couple of stalls yesterday and on the second one I ended up in a dive and my instructor had to take over. He said I was getting along fine except for my throttle coordination. My turns and banks are perfect. When I am up I seem to forget everything and my mind is on handling that ship. The other day we climbed up above the clouds and it was so pretty up there I wanted to get out and walk.

It's another weekend here and we will be off in a few hours. I hope to get in some shopping tonight since I am a little burdened with some money due to payday last Tuesday. I better close now and get ready to go out to the field. I'll write again soon and in the meantime you all keep praying for me and I love all of you forever. My picture will be ready soon.

Captain Johnny Ingram. U.S.A.A.F.

Monday

Hello folks,

I haven't got much time but I will attempt a few lines. I'll tell you the truth, I hardly have time to think. Right now I should be working on my flight notes and if I get caught writing this I catch the devil. The only time you are really able to write is on Sunday, the rest of your spare time you are supposed to be studying.

I had a nice weekend and Sunday I had a date with a very nice blonde and a bunch of us went on a little outing out at the park. I ate so much watermelon that I thought I was going to cut loose before I could ever get back to the college.

We didn't fly today due to a 45 mile an hour north wind but it has slacked up now and we are scheduled to go up at 7:30 tomorrow morning. I didn't have such a good day last Saturday because it was rough again but I am hoping for a good day tomorrow. My instructor says I am doing fine but you never can tell.

I hope everything is well and happy because I am. Tell everybody hello for me and I'll write again soon. Pray for me because I gotta make it.

Love,

Son

P.S. I got my flashlight today and you spoiled me. I look for a package every week now.

Monday

Hello folks,

Man this army is a messed up affair. I just got straightened out and it is the fourth time I've moved since I've been here. 250 new men came in this evening and they up and moved us overto the next building. It looks like this time next week I'll be headed for California. We have our graduation dance Friday night and then it's just a matter of a few days.

I had my check ride today, makes my ninth trip up. Tomorrow we will work on spins and stalls. I took off and landed it today for the second time. I am landing, which is the hardest and most nerve breaking thing about flying. I never ever give it a thought until I have set her down and turned her up to the hangar then I get that burning in my stomach.

I am sending that picture I promised you. I just got it today and if I get through Santa Ana I'll get a 100 made.

I've got to quit now and drop Ed Mock a line before I start studying. I got a letter from him today and he says he's going to have his 8th operation soon. Tell everybody hello and lookout for a call this week.

Love,
Son

Wednesday

Hello folks,

It certainly was good to hear all of you tonight. Maybe I can call you again before I leave. LaMarr really tickled me, I can't picture him now since I've heard him talk.

We have our dance tomorrow night instead of Friday and it looks like we will ship out Saturday. I sure do hate to leave this place. They say we will be on the train for about three days going out to California. I hope we get Pullmans this time. I don't believe I could fight another ride in those cattle cars we had coming out here.

This Santa Ana deal is really on my mind. I gotta get through it and if I do I can't decide what I want to be. Me and the Lord will think of something though.

I better close now and walk over to get my pay book signed before lights go out. I will also get my shot record which is complete and I certainly will be glad to see that. Keep on writing, I will get it wherever I go.

Good night and pray for me

Love,

Son

This letter also had a newspaper clipping called daily verse

Daily verse

Be with him, Lord

Be with him, Lord, on his precious way,

For danger hide upon the bomb-swept road

Walk with him in the start of every day,

Bring him back safely to his rude abode

Stay close to him when doubt and deepest wow

Attend him, be his food and drink should he be

Cast into the wilderness with no resource beside his ingenuity

Be with him, Lord and keep before his eyes

A vision of high honor, the reward of a clear conscience

And the sweet surprise of a safe journey home

Be with him, Lord!

Saturday 1 o'clock

Hello folks,

Well everything is set and we ship out this evening. I have all my stuff packed and I'm ready to go but I'm not too happy over leaving this place. Maybe it's because of the suspense I'm in about Santa Ana and classification.

We have Pullmans on the way out. I have made some nice friends here and I certainly hate to go but it was the same way at Kessler.

You all keep writing to me, just send it to this address and I will get it wherever I go.

If I can write, I'll write as soon as I get there. Keep your fingers crossed for me and pray for me because this is it. The big test is whether you can pin those wings and bars on me or not.

Love and kisses,

Son

SEPTEMBER 29, 1943 - JANUARY 4, 1944

SANTA ANA, CA
(PRE-FLIGHT)

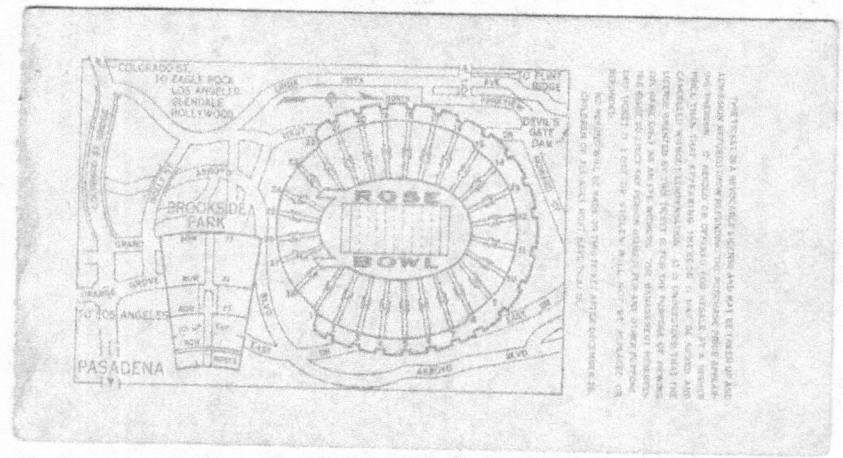

ticket stub from the Rose Bowl

9/28/43 *(Written by the commanding officer)*

Dear Mother,

I'm sending this from the Classification Center here at the Santa Santa Army Air Base, where I arrived today. I was met at the train and I am now here with the rest of the future Army Air crews.

I've been registered and assigned to Squadron 7, where I'll shall remain for about two weeks. During that time, I will have my physical examinations and tests which will determine whether I become a Pilot, Bombardier, or Navigator. After being classified, I will be assigned to another squadron here on the post, and then my actual pre-flight training begins. That pre-flight training will last about nine weeks and then I will be sent to one of the flying schools to start my flying training.

You will, no doubt, think it strange receiving this type of letter from me instead of a personal note, but here is why: our Commanding Officer knows that during the excitement and process of getting settled during the next few days, some of us will be apt to forget to write the folks at home. This is his way of letting you know where I am and I am well. It's just one of the many indications that I shall be well taken care of in the Army Air Forces. Another is my protection by National Service Life Insurance which is granted to me free of charge all through my training period.

I know I'll have more nice things to tell you when I write a real letter. In the meantime, please let me hear from you. My address is:

Squadron 7

Army Air Base

Santa Anna, CA

Thursday

Hello Folks,

Well here I am in sunny Cal. and they keep us on the run from 5:00 AM to 10:00 PM. Yes! It gets tougher and tougher as we go along. We thought it was tough back at Tech, but compared to this place, Tech was a vacation for us. We have 12 days of classification – we are on our second day now. Today we have an aptitude test all day. I'm just sitting tight and doing my best and praying that I'll get through. If I don't, it won't be because I haven't tried.

I am quarantined to the barracks for 14 days and restricted to the post for 42 days. So you see, I won't see much of Cal. for a long time. When they do let us out, I'm going to Los Angeles and if I have the money, I'll call. We had a good trip out here and I really saw some sites. We got on the train last Saturday about 5 PM and we got here Tuesday morning about 8:30. Well it's 7:03 now and we have inspection in five minutes, so I better close. You stick with me and let's hope I make it. Write every day, please!

Love and Kisses,

Son

Saturday

Hello Folks,

Well I thought I was really getting it tough these last 3 months, but compared to this place, it was just a picnic. Monday, I will finish up my test and then I'll just be hanging around with my fingers crossed waiting for the final word. We had part of our physical today along with a personal interview by a psychologist. He's the guy who finds out what kind of guy you are and your general attitude. He sure did ask me some deep and VERY personal questions, but I guess he knows what he is doing. Some were pretty embarrassing, but I told him the truth.

Some of the fellows have washed out already and they take it pretty hard. The boy that sleeps next to me washed out today because he fainted during a blood test. I'm taking everything as they come and doing my best. If I do flunk out, it won't be because I haven't tried.

I got a letter from HG today and he really has it easy – he works 12 hours and is off 24. Sometimes I wonder whatever made me get into this kind of training. I stay in a strain all the time trying not to make a mistake. I won't regret it if you all can pin those wings on me someday.

I can't tell you much about this place since I was asleep when I came in and we haven't been out of sight of the barracks. When I do get out (42 days from now), I'll have enough money to take in Los Angeles, Hollywood, and the rest of the sites here.

I hope you are all fine. The last letter I got from you was written the day before I called you back at Tech. Tell everybody hello for me and write.

Well, I gotta stop now and start scrubbing the floor for inspection tomorrow. Yes, tomorrow is Sunday, but to an a/c (air cadet), it's just another day. We have inspection and parade tomorrow. If I ever do get home, I'm going to bed and sleep for about five days.

You all write as often as you can and send them airmail (they get here in two days that way). Also, send me some airmail stamps cause I can't get out to buy any. Good night now and pray for me.

Love,

Son

Tuesday

Hello Folks,

Well, I've been here a week today and I've hustled every minute. I finished up all the classification tests yesterday and I'm just sitting tight until they tell me how I came out. Quite a few have washed out already and I guess there will be more later. I had a complete physical yesterday and instead of making a big noise over my knee and ankle, they let me go and took a ½ dozen x-rays of my elbow I broke about 10 years ago. I hope they don't show anything wrong. I have applied for a pilot for my first choice and bombardier for my second and if I qualify, I get what I asked for. Pilot training is a long, hard road. I don't know whether I should have chosen it or not, but after those 10 hours at the stick back in Texas, that's what I want.

I'm confined for 42 days. That's gonna be the toughest thing about this place. I figured it up yesterday and I've had a grand total of five days and four nights off since I've been in this Air Corps. In the regular army, they have every night free and also the weekends, but if you are a potential officer of the US Army Air Corps, they make you good little boys by keeping you in all the time. I got a few little trinkets for you all when we stopped in New Mexico to eat on the way out and when I get time, I'll send them.

Hurry up and write all of you and please send them by airmail so I can get them quicker. Also send me some airmail stamps cause I can't get out to get any. I ran out of paper so I'll quit now and write again later. Remember me in your prayers and keep your fingers crossed for me.

Love and Kisses,

Son

Thursday

Hello Folks,

I just got time for a few lines tonight. I've got KP for 16 hours tomorrow and I'll have to get more than a good night's sleep to make it tomorrow.

I've had a bad cold for the last two days. If I go on sick call, they'll lay me up in the hospital for a couple of weeks and call it pneumonia. I can just doctor myself the best I can and keep going. I'm going to take another big dose of medicine tonight.

Well, all three of my roommates that were with me at Tech have washed out. So far about 60 have washed and more are coming. I had a real scare this evening. I was called up before the board today at 1:15 and I sat up at headquarters on the waiting bench for three hours in a cold sweat. It turned out to be an error about my education that had to be straightened out and I was relieved. It really takes a darn good man to get through this and I'll tell you right now, I'll consider myself lucky and blessed if I make it. Only four more days to sweat out.

I hope everything is going fine at home. I sure would like to get back to see the place just to refresh my mind a little. It's tough on an ole home lover like me. I'm still the same though. The cut-up of the whole squadron.

Mom, hurry up and write and make everyone else drop me a line. Remember me in your prayers and I'll keep on giving it all I got.

Love and Kisses for all,

Son

Saturday

Hello Folks,

The last three days have been tough sailing for me. Thursday it was a 20 mile hike to the mountains and back. Friday it was 18 hours of KP. Today it was the firing range and tonight it is guard duty. I go on guard at 12:00 tonight and get off at 4:00 in the morning. I'm in the guardhouse now laying around until the time comes. I reckon it sounds like I'm taking basic over again. Well basic wasn't like this. We have finished our classification and now we get all the dirty work until Tuesday when they tell us whether we make it or not.

You ask me to explain this classification to you. Well, the three months that I spent at Keesler and Texas were supposed to be getting me ready for this. This is where you really get down to business. I took about 25 different kinds of examinations, including a physical. They will, according to my grades, then classify me as a bombardier, pilot, or navigator according to what I am best suited for. They washed five more of my buddies today and it's rumored that a big list goes up tomorrow morning. I just pray to the good Lord that I'm not on it. Tuesday is the big day. This is the day we are made cadets - if we get through and are issued cadet clothing. Let's all pray that I make it.

I'm glad Dad likes his jacket I sent him. Tell him it's a real G.I.. It was issued to me when I came in and I knew I was going to have to turn it back in when I came out here, so I got a girl back at school to mail it for me. It's really a nice jacket and will come in handy this winter.

I got your letter this morning. The first that was mailed after you got my Gl. (the typewritten one). Tell LaMarr to write to me again. We all laughed at his last letter.

I got a stack of newspapers today a foot high. It was some that had accumulated at Tech. I don't get a chance to read them when they come in like that, but I cover them the best I can. Start your letters rolling as soon as you can.

I'm just up and down all the time. Sometimes I really get fed up with it. I'm afraid if I ever get out, I'll be an old man and I have spent the best years of my life locked up in an army camp. This thing really hit me fast and I still can't believe it's really me sometimes.

They really have a time with us. We are all just a young bunch of kids and everything we do, we play at it. There's nothing we really take seriously. I wish this thing would hurry up and get over with.

Well, I better stop and get a little sleep before I go on duty. Write often and pray for me cause I gotta make it.

Love and Kisses, Son

Tuesday

Hello Folks,

Well, it's all over now and I was classified as a pilot!! We had a sort of graduation exercise at noon and then they told us what we were classified as. I am really glad it's all over and it takes a load off my mind. These last 12 days have really been tough ones and I feel a little relaxed.

My class is all split up now. Some may be bombardiers and others navigators. The navigators are shipping out tomorrow, but the bombardiers will go to ground school along with us pilots. From now on it really counts and the hard work is yet to come. It takes a good man plus all the luck and brakes he can get to get through this pilot training. I wanted pilot training. I asked for it and got it, so from here on the question is, can I take it and will I get the breaks. Let's all hope so because I really want it.

Our squadron doesn't start ground school till November 1. We are supposed to go on a 2 week backpack in the mountains while we are waiting to go to school. I hope we get to go. I need a couple of weeks to rest in the mountains.

Well, after tonight we can go most anywhere on the post and one night when I have time I'll run over and have a picture taken in my cadet uniform. We can wear officer clothes (except the pinks) now and also officer insignias.

I had to leave y'all for a while to stand retreat but I'm back now and my knees are still shaking. One of the wing officers was absent tonight and I took his place in the retreat parade. I had to march out in front of the 3 squadrons of our wing along with 2 other student officers. Man, I gave the major a salute when we passed in review, and that liked to have knocked him down. We won the review for the 2nd straight night.

I'm slowly and gradually getting in the habit of this kind of life and I don't think so much of wanting to go home like I used to. I've almost forgotten how home looks which will make the day I get back much happier.

Well, I better stop now and get busy cleaning up around here. Today was a great day for all of us and the barracks sure look like it too. Tell everybody I made it and also to write me. You all write as often as you can and I will every chance I get. Remember me in your prayers and so long for now.

Love and Kisses,

a/c Johnny - Son

Hello Folks,

I was in the pressure chamber all morning for a test flight to see how I reacted to high altitude flying. As you know, the amount of oxygen in the air at 15,000 feet makes it impossible for a guy to live over 5 minutes, and in this war very little flying is done below this altitude. All pilots today have to use an oxygen mask above 10,000 feet. Well this morning, we were taken up to different altitudes in the pressure chamber to see if we could take it. I went to 35,000 feet before I passed out which proved that I could stand it. We remained at 30,000 feet for an hour with oxygen and most everybody lasted. It was a lot of fun and we all enjoyed watching each other turn blue, get groggy, and then topple over. It hit me the same as it did everybody else. I kept writing my name and serial number and each time I wrote my writing was a little worse until long toward the end, when it had almost overcome me, I was doing nothing but scribbling and I thought I was writing my name. We get tests like that all the time and some that are really fun.

Well, I don't guess you all will hear from me anytime next week. We leave Sunday for the mountains (walking) on a 7 day stay out in the open under battle conditions. You know sleeping in foxholes and not shaving or bathing. I'll have a lot to tell you when I get back. You'all keep writing to me so I'll have lots of mail waiting for me when I get back. I'm glad you (Mom) and LaMarr had a good time in Greensboro. Makes me think of the trip you took last summer when I was working and how Evelyn liked to have starved me and Dad to death.

I'm getting my papers OK now and they do almost as much good as a letter. It looks like anybody can get in the Air Corps now. I guess they can, but the big question is staying in. We all had a good laugh the other day at a column in the Herald about some of the boys leaving for Keesler field where they will begin preflight training as Aviator Cadets. The poor boys don't know it, but they are nothing but buck privates and won't be cadets or go into preflight till 7 months from now, and then 1/4 of them will wash out before they get to classification and get a chance to become cadets. I'm a full-fledged cadet now (Thank God) just beginning my preflight and I am 4 months ahead of schedule.

I'm still looking forward to getting to LA when they let us out and we've only got 26 more days to go. Well, I better close now and get ready for chow. I'll write again before I leave Sunday. All of you write. Keep smiling and pray for me.

Love and Kisses, Son

(PS - I'm having another picture made now in my cadet uniform with all the brass, and also in flying togs)

Saturday

Hello Folks,

I guess you've been wondering what has become of me. I'm safe and sound but I'm fed up with the hills and I'm ready to go back to the base. I think I told you that we don't start ground school till November 1 which gives us about three weeks with nothing to do. But that doesn't stop the big boys, they trucked us 25 miles up here in the mountains and we've been here since last Sunday. We sleep out on the ground under the stars and eat K rations half the time. Nevertheless, it's a beautiful place with a nice lake and all we do is lay around in the sun, swim or play any kind of sports. It rained the first day we were here and all my stuff got wet, including my stationary so I've been without any writing material ever since.

Do you remember Mrs. Ezell over on Buchanan? If you see her, you tell her I'm up here with her brother Jimmy. We sleep together and fight over the covers all night.

HG sent me a good picture of himself and I also heard from Aunt Ethel. I'll have some pictures made if I ever get back to the base. I got the snapshot yesterday and they kinda make me homesick, especially the one of Dad and the crew going off to work. The one of Evelyn and LaMarr at church had me baffled. I didn't know either one of them. Hildo has a good looking girlfriend too.

I wish you could be here with me right now. I'm sitting up here on the very tip top of a mountain in a pair of underwear shorts and the scenery is just like you see in the movies. I'm so high up that the Pacific Ocean can be seen easily. We go back to the base tomorrow and walk. I know I'll be dead tired tomorrow night.

I still get the paper and all of us NC boys read it from the front to the rear without missing a thing. I've also got quite a tan since I've been up here. It's 100° here in the daytime and feels like below zero at night.

Mom, you say you don't know what to send me, well I'll tell you what really hits the spot and is always welcome - cookies and candy is the best thing. It looks like I never get enough to eat and that would be the answer.

Well, I better close now, grab my mess kit, and hit the chow line. I'll write again soon. Pray for me and all of you take good care of yourselves.

Love and Kisses, Aviation Cadet, Johnny Ingram 346075159

Monday

Hello Folks,

Here I am sitting in the service club. It's 7:45 now and I got an appointment with the dentist at 8:30 to ease my mind a little. I thought I would drop you a line.

I don't know what has got to be done to my teeth, but I hope they don't decide to pull all of them out.

Well, I'm back at the base now and I guess I will start school in about two weeks. I wish they'd hurry up and start us. These details will kill you.

I got LaMarr's letter today and the boys posted it up on the bulletin board right beside the Lt's orders of the day. They got a big kick out of it.

I signed two payrolls out in the mountains, so I guess we'll be getting a little of that G.I. salad in a few days and maybe a weekend off soon. I really need a little of that fresh air.

Well, I better run down to the coal miner and let him start drilling. You know how I dread a dentist. Say a little prayer for me and take care of yourselves.

Good night all,

Son

Saturday

Hello Folks,

I've been a bad little boy and I have paid for it. I'm surprised that I hadn't messed up long ago. I didn't do anything so drastic - it just proves the things we have to put up with. Last Tuesday night they called us out for a formation to get paid at 9:45 o'clock - 15 minutes till taps. I was in bed asleep and missed the formation. Well, when the boys came back, they woke me up and I ran over to the orderly room to explain. But as usual I had to say "no excuse sir" along with nine other guys and we all got five days KP, 4:45 to 8:30 every day. For good behavior and attitude, the Lt. knocked off a day of it so I don't have to go tomorrow. It's just an everyday thing so don't get alarmed over it. We go over to pre-flight school Tuesday and I sure will be glad of it. We are already taking code and I like it. As for you all coming to see me for Xmas, I guess you'll have to cancel it cause at that time I'll be on my way somewhere else. We are supposed to have 8 weeks of preflight and since we start this week, we will be getting out the last part of December. Besides, it's a long trip and there is no place to stay out here and also I would only get to see very little of you. I guess we'll just have to wait. It couldn't hurt. I'll just make it twice as good to see you the longer we wait.

I guess you have noticed the way my writing has dropped off, but with all of this stacked up on us, I just don't have the time and it will even be worse after next week cause I'll be going to classes clear up to 8:30 at night. Don't you slack off cause I look for letters as much as I do bedtime and I can't make it without them.

Snooky - the little girl I was stepping out with when I was in Texas - sent me a big box of cookies the other day and I really am enjoying them. Eats like that are about the only thing I need.

I heard from grandmother too and I am going to write to her the next time I get a chance. I still get my papers and I get homesick every time I get a big fat Sunday paper. I don't know why but I do.

Well, I better sign off now and get to bed. That KP has just about cooked my goose. Keep writing and all of you take good care of yourselves. I'd like a furlough but I don't want it to be an emergency furlough. Keep your fingers crossed for me - say a little prayer for me and I'll be thinking of you.

Love and Kisses,

Son

PS - I'm sorry you'all got mixed up on the officer uniform. I don't wear the bars of course, but the cadet issue is similar to the officers. I'll send you a picture soon and it will explain everything. The dentist and I are still having it out – ouch!

Tuesday

Hello Folks,

I got another letter from you today. I just posted LaMarr's little note on the bulletin board. The other boys think his letters are so newsy and they are planning on sending it to the headquarters recommending it as a new type of secret code.

Well, we go to preflight tomorrow and the sooner we get out of that, the better it will be. This will be the last bit of bookwork we'll have to do and from then on out I'll be flying. There is also a possibility that I will get home for Xmas. Don't bank on that too strongly cause I'm not. But since Xmas will catch us between preflight and primary, there is a good possibility. Let's hope and pray they give us a few days.

You asked about recreation. Well there is very little here and besides we go to classes up till bedtime and we have very little recreation.

Yep, me and the dentist are really having it out. He gets everything pretty much his way, though. I got to have a few wisdom teeth yanked. The army says you can't fly with your wisdom teeth.

Well, I better close now. We get paid again sometime this afternoon. That's the way they do it – you go for months and they up and pay it all at one time. This makes the second payday in two weeks. Well so long for now, pray for me and keep writing.

Love and Kisses to all,
Little John

11/8/43
Saturday

Hello Folks,

I've been here in preflight now for a week and no kidding this is the first chance I've had to sit down. I've thought we had taken just about all they could dish out but it seems that they double it every time.

We start classes at 6:45 AM believe it or not, right up till bedtime as hard as we can. The studies are interesting but it's the little crap you have to put up with that kills you. We are learning code radio, naval ships and planes, math of course, physics, military hygiene, and gunnery. We have about 6 or 7 weeks then the big time, primary, yep we fly from then on out (I hope and pray).

The dentist is still on my teeth. We have to have our wisdom teeth pulled. I think I'll only have to have one.

Mom, if you can, find out where Hall and the bunch are and let me know. I'd like to know if they're being pushed through this stuff as fast as I am. I got a little money saved up now for next weekend (we get off I hope). Since we got our raise, I am buying a bond ($25) every month. If I get through this alive, I ought to have a little money to carry me through the depression – eh!

Well, I hope you are all well and get enough sleep. Lord knows I don't. Only seven hours a night. Remember how healthy you said I'd be if I've got plenty of rest. The army doesn't think so.

I'm going to church tomorrow and afterwards I'll drift over and have my picture made for you. I weigh 150 lbs now but I still have room for more. At this rate or routine we are on now, I guess I'll lose all of it.

Well, I better sign off now and hit the sack. I can hardly hold my eyes open now. Write every day and I hope things will kinda slack up soon so I'll be able to write like I'd like to. Kiss LaMarr for me and all of you keep smiling and praying for me cause I'm too deep in it now to quit.

Love and bear hugs to you all from your son - John H Jr.

11/12/43

Hello Folks,

Hi, I just got back from the dentist. One more trip and I'll be through. I found out tonight that I won't have to have any pulled, so that's a big relief. I got a swell dentist. In fact we get the best. The regular enlisted men's dentist clinics are mostly non-coms and student docs, but we go to the officers clinic and regular officer dentists work on us so we get the best there is. I've had 3 fillings and the next one will be all.

Well, I'm still plugging away and I'm beginning to get used to this 17 hour schedule. We still go to classes at 6:45 AM and bedtime still catches us in a study hall. The studies so far aren't so tough except for math. I really have to get down and dig for that stuff. Saturday is the big day folks, yep, after 8 long weeks of confinement and I get off this weekend. I was kinda surprised that I didn't get but one gig. Oh yeah, I forgot to tell you about the gig system. Well, for every little thing out of order they give you a gig. 8 gigs and you have to walk a tour (1 hour of walking) and every gig over 8 you walk one tour. The catch is you have to walk off your tours on the weekend and 4 tours will confine you for the weekend. (75 gigs will wash you out). It's nothing to get 20 gigs a week. I guess my buddies and I will go to Hollywood in Los Angeles for the weekend. I'll tell you all about it when I get back.

I heard from HG yesterday. He's going to grandad's this weekend to meet Aunt Ethel. He says also that he's got another stripe coming. Good boy, looks like he'll be an officer before I will. I got the slip to get your package, it's insured so I'll have to go over to the PO tomorrow to get it. I'd like it no matter what's in it. Cookies are my favorite (hint, hint).

Well, I'll sign off now and drop Mutt a line to kinda cheer him up. He doesn't like this army (nobody does). Be good all of you – say a little prayer for me and write when you can.

Love and Kisses - Son

Hi Evelyn,

I got a little space here so I'll drop you a line. Naturally I enjoy your letters more than you know. You kinda know all the news about what's left of the gang and who's doing what now. I wish you could be here this weekend to take in Hollywood and the big city with me. I'm going to see Henry James, he's at the Palladium, Ciro's and the Brown Derby where all the stars hang out. Also the Hollywood Canteen and maybe dance with Hedy LaMarr. I hear from the gang every once in a while. I don't do a very good job of answering them due to the fact that I don't have time, write often gal, and tell everyone hello for me.

Love, JH

Tell Ma Gholson I said hello and tell her the skins haven't forgotten her.

11/18/43
Wednesday

Hello Folks,

I just got time to say hello and I'm still here. Been getting your letters OK and the candy couldn't be better. Well I'm still getting it rough. Doing OK on all my studies so far except math and you can't imagine what they are throwing at us in that. The days are still crowded with a million things to do and of course the days aren't long enough for it all.

Got off last weekend and went to Hollywood. Took in all the hot spots and danced with Betty Davis at the Canteen! We stayed at the Y Saturday night and went to Long Beach Sunday morning with a Lt. from Lynchburg, VA. Had a big time there and I hope to get back there this weekend if I can go all day tomorrow without getting any more gigs. I got gigged something terrible this week because my hair was too long (so they say), so I went to the barber last night and got my head practically shaved. It is so short – well it's just a fuzz.

I went to the dentist again today (I don't mind it at all now) and he said one more trip will finish me up. He only does very little at a time. I gotta quit now before the lights go out on me. Nite, nite. Pray for me and keep writing.

Love, Son

If everything works out OK, I get my wings in June so save your money cause I want you all to pin them on me. I hope! I hope! I hope!

Nov. 22, 1943
Sunday night

Hello Folks,

Well, if I don't write to you all tonight I won't get another chance till next Sunday. I hope all of you are well and happy. I seem to be so at the moment but sometimes I get awful fed up with this. My back and legs ache and I can hardly hold my eyes open. I honestly believe if I didn't want to fly as bad as I do that I'd just tell them to cram the whole works.

Yesterday was exam day and we took a test in every subject that we have. I made 95 on my gunnery and I haven't heard from the others yet. If I didn't make any careless mistakes, I am expecting a good grade on math. Well, I went back to the big city again this weekend and I think I'll make that the last time; I've covered it well now and saw everything. It's really too wild and there's only about 1,000,000 soldiers, sailors, and marines raising cane.

Sure enough, it looks like Christmas is coming soon and naturally it won't be the same for me. I don't know what I want. In this outfit they tell you what you can have and what you can't have. I do have trouble shaving though – no soap, no blades – can't buy any. So if you can find me a good electric razor, it would be most appreciated.

Well, I better sign off now and get full advantage of those 7 hours. Be sweet all of you and pray for me.

Love and Kisses,

Little Johnny

I'm through with the dentist and my teeth are in top shape!

11/27/1943
Friday nite

Hello Folks,

I gotta make this a fast one, it's about time for lights out and I'm pretty well caught up with my work. I just got out of a math study hall. I got an 85 average in math, but I better not stop at that. When you get where everything is going OK and you're just tops and everything, that's when you better watch for something to bust wide open. So I went over it for a couple of hours tonight for good measure. Well, I'll be a little late getting out tomorrow night. I got two tours to walk before I can go. Can you believe it? It's been six months now and I'll walk my first tour tomorrow night. I'll be through by 8:00 though and if I feel like it, I guess I'll go into LA.

Next week we'll be upperclassmen and also get paid. The weeks seem to be passing pretty fast and it won't be long before we'll be in primary. I'd rather fly than study. I think Gordon Whitted and the boys are out here now. Yes see they were in Sqdn 606 at Keesler and I was in 600. I shipped to TX and about 3 weeks later, they shipped to SC. The boys tell me now that the old 606 is out here now in Sqdn 22 awaiting preflight. The schools were too crowded back east so they shipped them from TN out here. I'm going over tomorrow night to see if I can find them. I sure would like to see someone from home. Thanksgiving was just another day here. We worked, had a big turkey supper and I ate so much I'd like to have popped. I hope I can thank the Lord for a pair of wings next Nov. I better close now and doctor myself. I got a little cold, but I have some pills that are fixing me right up.

Love and kisses to all of you! Pray for me and look for a call from me soon. (about Sunday noon)

JH

12/9/1943

Hello Everybody,

I'm still here, healthy as ever and my morale isn't too low. I guess you wonder sometimes just what could keep me so busy that I couldn't write. You'll just have to bear with me in my letters folks cause I'm still on the move 16 hours a day for 6 days a week and I can't find time to write.

I'm moved again - they moved us from Sqdn 35 in the 1st wing to Sqdn 68 over here in the 4th wing and here I hope we'll stay until we ship to primary. Two more weeks folks and we'll turn our books in and what a glorious day that will be! No kidding, I've never studied so hard and constantly in all my life as I have here. First, it was math that had me by the throat. I finished that up with a 90 average and now it's physics, which is worse. I guess you all have troubles of your own though without having to listen to mine. It does seem unfair to me for a guy as young as I am to have such a load on me. Did I say young? I just remembered tomorrow is my birthday. Honestly, I never gave it a thought. Happy birthday to you too, Sis. I guess I'll celebrate with my nose in a stack of books and charts. I got your packages and they were the tops. I like my robe and it sure came just in time. I was going to get me one this weekend.

Well, they gave us the lowdown on Xmas holidays yesterday. We get all day Saturday, Saturday night, and Sunday up till 9:00. Seems mighty little to me but there's nothing I can do about it. I almost forgot, Mac McCullen came up last weekend from San Diego and we spent the weekend together at Long Beach. We sure did have a time talking about home. He couldn't get over all this crap we go through. We are going to try to get together for Xmas. I hope so anyway. Well, how is everything at home? If I ever get home again, don't be surprised if I look like a lost cause. I think of you lots and look forward to the day when I can see you. I hope LaMarr doesn't grow too fast. I guess Dad is still struggling with his latrine business. I'm looking for him to retire anytime now.

I hope the new year will find me in primary. I love flying, but I can't say much for this schooling. You sure have to know a lot to be a flyer. If I can just stay on the ball and not break under the strain, I think I'll make it and you'll never know how bad I want this. Most of the guys eliminate themselves. They get discouraged and fed up with it.

I've just about run out of news. It's the same thing here day in and day out and it's really hard to find things to write about. I don't hear from any of the gang much. In fact, I've dropped all correspondence since I don't have the time. I'm not sending any girl a line. The blonde bomber writes me about once a month. I guess she thinks she's still keeping me on the string. It's right funny. Well folks I'd better close now and study a while. I got two exams tomorrow. I'll keep on giving it all I got and you all keep praying for me. They've got me mad now and this is one thing I'm going to get through if I never do anything else in my life. Good night folks! Keep well and happy and don't worry about me.

All my love, John H. Jr. (yep. I'll spend my 19th birthday in the army).

12/17/1943
Thursday

Hello Everybody,

Just one more week to go and I'll graduate from this phase
of the long hard road. We finish classes next Thursday and I am
hoping I can finish with a good showing. The reason I haven't
written lately is due to the big rush to finish up. It's been exams
on top of exams – two and three a day and it's kept me right in
those books.

There's a big flu and spinal meningitis epidemic going on
out here mostly due to this crazy CA weather. Last Sunday, they
gave us four huge sulfur dyesol pills to keep the mutations out of
us and now we get our bunks separated from each other by a bug
sheet hanging between each bunk to keep from spreading the flu
around. I got a touch of it myself, a bad cold, and I really pour
the medicine down every night. Everything I can get my hands
on. I've been feeling pretty low all week but I think I'll pull
through. Everytime I get to feeling bad I want to go home.

I got the packages OK and I like my razor and robe the
best. I'm going to try to get some things home to y'all for Xmas if
I can. I am so pushed for time that actually, well it's hard to
explain, I just don't have any spare time.

I hope Xmas will go well with you. I'm going to sleep
myself. The whole base is taking off for Xmas, so I guess we'll (fly
buddies and I) get us a room somewhere with good mattresses,
sheets, and sleep till my hearts content. Boy this training is the

kind that you wouldn't give a million dollars for after you get through and you couldn't be paid a million dollars to go through it all again.

I got a few Xmas cards so far and I'm planning on getting mine out this weekend. I'm all for them kicking Holton and Warren out of the school. I bet it's really getting hot around there.

Well, I better close now since there is really no good news from here. Be sweet all of you – take care of yourselves and pray for me because I gotta make it.

Good night and write soon,

Love, Son

12/21/1943
Sunday night

Hello Folks,

I thought I'd drop you a line tonight since I won't have time to write during the week. This is supposed to be the last week. This is supposed to be the last week here and I can see right now that it'll be the longest of them all.

I thought I'd get in some shopping this weekend so I took off to Long Beach - started in and out of the stores and before I could decide what I wanted, the stores closed on me. Well we came back to the base and I thought I'd try to get a good night's sleep, get up early and finish my Xmas shopping, etc. Well, I didn't wake up till 2:00 PM so that was sunk. Then I had to go to school tonight and well, 5:00 AM starts another week tomorrow. So you can see just how much spare time I have even on the weekend.

You wouldn't know it was Christmas around here except for the carols playing over the radio. We will break out and sing one once in a while. This is going to be a quiet Christmas for us.

Well, my cold is a lot better. I got me some capsules and they just about knocked it out of me. It's still raining out here and it's scheduled to keep it up till Feb.

We got wind today that we would get one day for New Year's so that'll help a lot too. I'm gonna try to get me a ticket to the Rose Bowl over at Pasadena for that day. That's about all from here. Really no news at all... Same thing every day. Have a big Christmas and say a little prayer for me.

Love & Kisses,

Little John

Tell LaMarr I hope Santa Claus is good to him.

Hello Folks,

Lord! I sure have been in one heck of a strain for the last three days and now it's over and I feel like just flopping right here in the middle of the floor! We were supposed to have our final exams next Friday, but they pulled some more crap on us and announced Wednesday that we would have all of our exams on Thursday night and Friday of this week.

We went to the beach range Tuesday and Wednesday night, then it was guard duty. Went to school last night and had all those exams today without time to look at a book. I burnt the flashlight you sent me clean out last night trying to study down at the latrine after taps. That's just one example of the daily crap we take. I'm in military hygiene class now, (we don't get tested on it) and the teacher (1st Lt.) has just up and admitted that he couldn't think of anything else to say. They take a good math teacher and put him to teaching medicine. Naturally, they don't know their twat from their elbow about it.

I got the money Mom and just in time too. I'll pay you back when we get paid the first of next month. We get off for our Xmas holidays in a couple of hours from now. It sure going to be swell having two straight days off. I sure will be thinking of home and all of you this Xmas. I bet LaMarr has the best Xmas of us all.

We have got our rooms in LA and I'm going to pile right up in bed as soon as I get there. It's rained all week here and my uniform looks like I slept in it so I'll have to get it pressed before

I can even show my face on the street. We sure had fun on the range last Tuesday. I fired just about everything the army had. I liked the 50 caliber machine gun best. Completely destroyed three targets with it.

Folks, let's hope and pray I pass those exams so I can get out of here to primary. They are holding lots of boys over for low average. If I come out on top, I'll move to primary in a week or two. Pray for me. Keep those fingers crossed and I miss all of you most at Christmas.

Love and Kisses,

John H.

I hope I can spend next Christmas at home.

Excuse this beautiful stationary. I'm in class and it's the only thing I got. Merry Xmas and victorious new year.

12/26/1943
Monday

Hello folks,

Well Xmas is over and I feel as though it was just another weekend for me. We got into LA about 5 PM Friday evening and checked in the hotel. There were about 25 or 30 of us from our sqdn all on the same floor and since it was the top floor, we kinda let loose. Some of the boys had their wives with them. We went out and bought us a little tree and the wives, with our help, decorated the tree. We all stayed up till the wee hours of Xmas morning talking and laughing about the crap we have to take here. The wives were good sports and I think everybody enjoyed the little time together. Well, from then on out I did almost nothing but sleep and enjoyed every wink so I really don't know how Christmas was this year, cause I slept through it.

Well, I feel so much at ease tonight. We got all our grades today and I came out rather good on all of them. I had a good 88 average in physics but I fell down on my last exam and I came out with a 75 average on that. The rest were above 88 and I figure I'll come out with about an 84 average for the whole works. Boy, it's a big load off my mind and I certainly feel swell now. We will probably ship to primary the first of the year if they don't hold us over on account of crowded primary schools.

I just enjoyed a nice hour reading my newspapers. I see where everybody's home from school for Xmas and I'd give a pretty penny to see them all. I have to laugh every time I think about the way those girls will put on the dog after a half year in college. I'll bet it'll be awful. Of course, they'll be too big for the crazy little things we used to do. I guess they think the same about me if I ever get my wings, but I don't think it'll ever happen to me.

I tried to call you over the holidays and it was "no soap." It's just impossible for me to call you from out here unless I had about a week to spend in a phone booth. It doesn't cost but $3.75 but I'm just going to have to wait for a lotta things that I want to do. The whole west coast is packed and jammed with people from all over the country and on weekends it's simply awful. The streets are so crowded that it takes a half an hour to even walk 3 or 4 blocks. I want to send all of you something for Xmas, but couldn't because the stores close at six and I don't get in until 6:30 or 7:00.

Well, I hope you all had a big Xmas and I'm hoping to be there next year. (I doubt it though). I'm signing off now and going to bed. Be sweet all of you – pray for me and write often.

Johnny (that's my G.I. name)

If you see any pictures in the news reels (movies) about the Rose Bowl game, look for me cause I'm going to be there next weekend – I'll be in the stands.

12/30/1943
Thursday

Happy New Year, Folks!

This is the way I like it now. We are all through and we just lay around and wait for the order to come through for us to ship out. The C.O. gave us a little dope on the situation today. He says he expects the orders in a few days but—— the primary schools are so crowded now that about 1400 of our class will be held over for another four weeks. The holdover will be based on academic averages and military behavior. My average is 85.14 and I have 35 gigs. I'm hoping I won't be held over. I seem to be pretty safe, but you never can tell. Enough said about that so I'll get on with my New Year's pass.

We get off tomorrow at 12:00 and have to be back on the base at 3:00 on Sunday. We planned a pretty big weekend – taking in the Rose Bowl game and Harry James at the Palladium. I can't help remembering the big time I had last year at the Xmas dances and all the gang. Most of them remembered me with a Christmas card and wanted to know when I'm coming home (that's a laugh). Tell Evelyn to drop me a line about the crowd.

Tell Dad I hope he makes a million dollars in '44. I'm hoping for a pair of wings and a good sound mind and body. Well, I better quit my rambling now and scrub under my bunk. G.I. Party tonight. Write often all of you – pray for me and I'll be thinking of you.

Love and Kisses,

G.I. John

I hope to go to Texas for primary ——

1/4/44
Monday

Greetings Folks,

And a happy new year. Well it's all said and done now and this time next week will find me in Phoenix, Ariz. – Thunderbird Field to be exact. The orders came through today and we are sure split up. The sqdn is broken up and we are going in all directions. Most of the guys drew small fields within about a 100 mile radius of here. If you remember the movie Thunderbird, that's where I'm going. It's out in the desert, the weather is fine, especially for flying, but it's rumored that they have the highest percent washout rate. That's an uncomfortable thought, but I'm going to try to make the best of it, stay on the ball, and I think I can make it.

My New Year's leave was just the opposite from the weekend Xmas. You know I slept through Xmas. Well this time I hardly got any sleep. We got into LA about 4:00 Friday – ate supper and took in the big New Year's celebration at the Palladium in Hollywood. Harry James was there and so was everybody else. We had a big time dancing and gazing at the movie stars.

Got up Saturday morning and went to Pasadena for the Rose Bowl game. Had good seats right on the 50 yard line. The bowl is beautiful, it's right between two high mountains. As for football, the game was pretty sloppy, but the color and everything that goes with it made up for it..

Had a date Sat. night and she was a knockout. She was another one of those girls who came to Hollywood to become a star, but she ended up as an auditor at MGM. Boy was she dressed — big silver fox fur coat and everything —truly a queen — nice too! Yep, that was my last weekend in the big city and truly the best I've spent since I've been here. Couldn't help but wish I was home though.

I don't guess you all made such a big to do over the new year, but out here the place went wild. I got your letter today, the one you wrote for Xmas and I thought I'd die over Mr. Stutts telling LaMarr that Santa Claus got run over. I sure would have liked to see him Xmas morning. So you saw the Blonde Bomber (working) — (it's a miracle). I thought she was good looking. You should see these Hollywood girls.

Well I better quit now, I've talked out and haven't said half as much as I want to. We ship Thursday morning, so I'll probably be kept busy for the rest of the week and I may not get a chance to write, but I will the minute I get there. Take good care of yourselves, Let's all pray that I make it and write often.

Love and Kisses,

John H

1/6/1944
Wednesday

Hello Folks,

Just a line before I shove-off. I've got everything packed and ready to go. We leave in the morning at 8:30 AM. I think I told you it's Thunderbird Field in Phoenix, Ariz. There's about 35 of us out of this sqdn going there. My three best buddies (one is the Knight boy, Mrs. Ezzels brother) are held over here for another month because their average wasn't high enough and I sure am going to miss them and those swell weekends we spent together in Hollywood. That's the way it's been though ever since I got in so we are all kinda used to it.

Well folks, I got that funny little feeling again just like I had when I came in here. It was a big test and I pulled through. This one is next and I will give it all I got. I know I can fly those crates cause I've done it, so I figure if I can stay on the ball and do my best, I'll weather the storm too. I'm too deep in it now and there's too many people pulling for me to drop out now.

Well I'll sign off now and log a little sack time (go to bed) because tomorrow is a big day. Be sweet all of you. Say a little prayer for me and write soon.

Love and Kisses,

G.I. Johnny

JANUARY 10 - MARCH 8, 1944

PHOENIX, AZ
THUNDERBIRD FIELD
(PRIMARY TRAINING)

Class 44-G annual
Thunderbird Field
Phoenix, Arizona

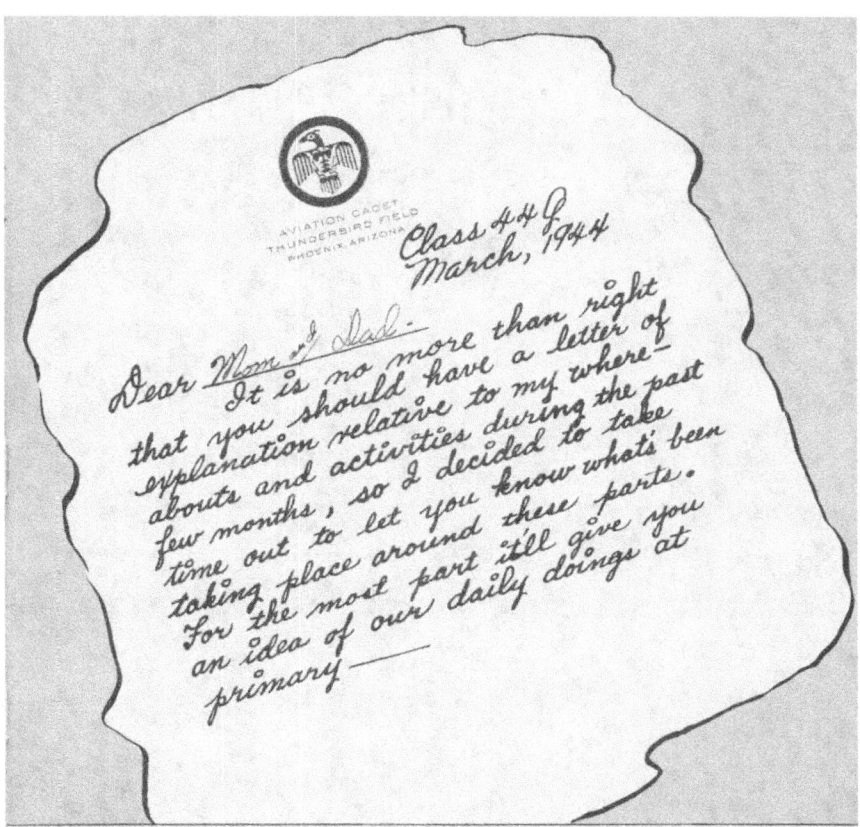

AVIATION CADET
THUNDERBIRD FIELD
PHOENIX, ARIZONA

Class 44 G
March, 1944

Dear Mom & Dad -

It is no more than right that you should have a letter of explanation relative to my where-abouts and activities during the past few months, so I decided to take time out to let you know what's been taking place around these parts. For the most part it'll give you an idea of our daily doings at primary —

We have come a long way and we are still in there pitching, having hurdled such tasks as Army basic training, C.T.D., the classification center, and the most complete and detailed preflight school in the world at Santa Ana, California. With such duties well performed we eagerly awaited our opportunities at Thunderbird No. 2 which lies in the desert sands of Arizona.

We are now future airmen of America, having completed our first stage toward becoming a part of the greatest All-American flying team in all history. We must win wings and with wings win battles of the skies. We have had moments of gladness and sorrow, moments of thrill and defeat, moments of toil and bewilderment too, but there's nothing like those moments that we had when we flew. Disappointments have spread themselves generously along our path but we have kept surging forward while others have fallen by the wayside thru no fault of their own.

Class 44-G annual
Thunderbird Field
Phoenix, Arizona
(continued)

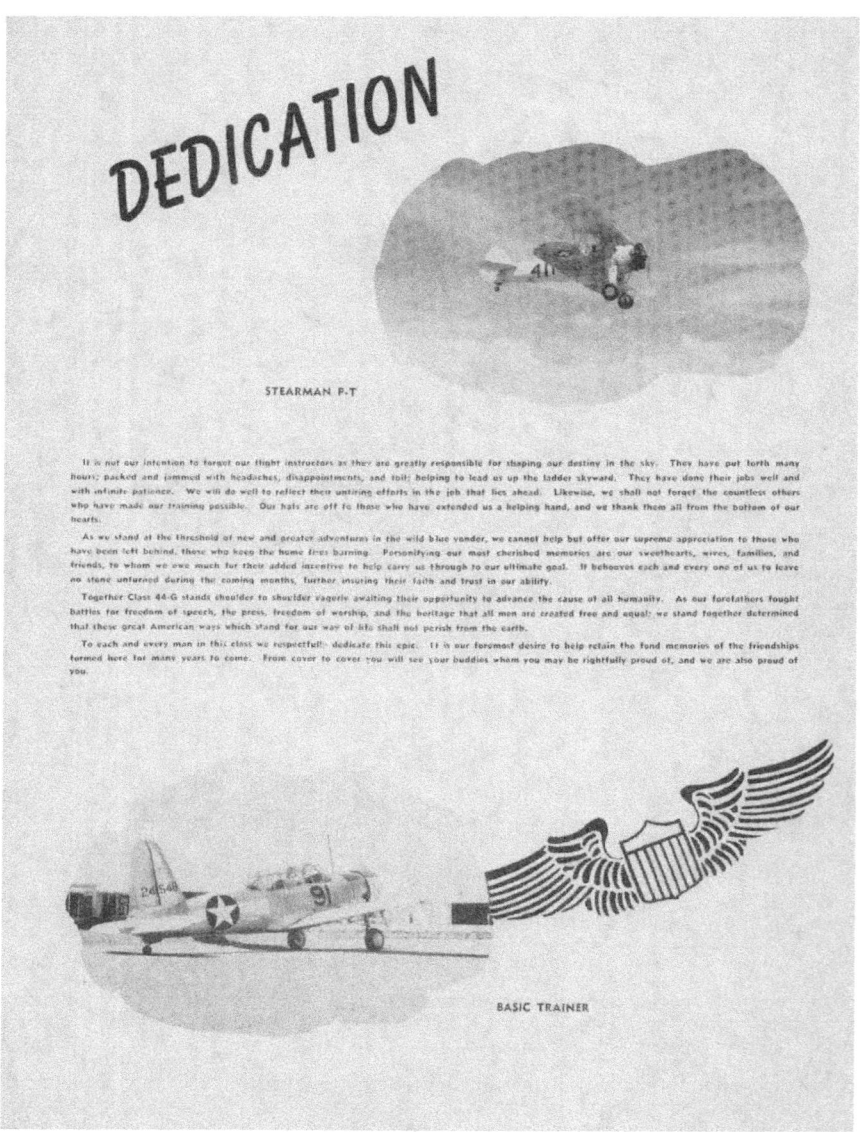

Class 44-G annual
Thunderbird Field
Phoenix, Arizona
(continued)

Stearman

(written on the back of the photo)
Left to right standing: a/c - R.B. Worthington, a/c - D.W. Johnson,
Instructor - G.E. Pallas, a/c - N.M. Kavanaugh
Left to right kneeling: a/c - J.H. Ingram, a/c - D.R. Keene

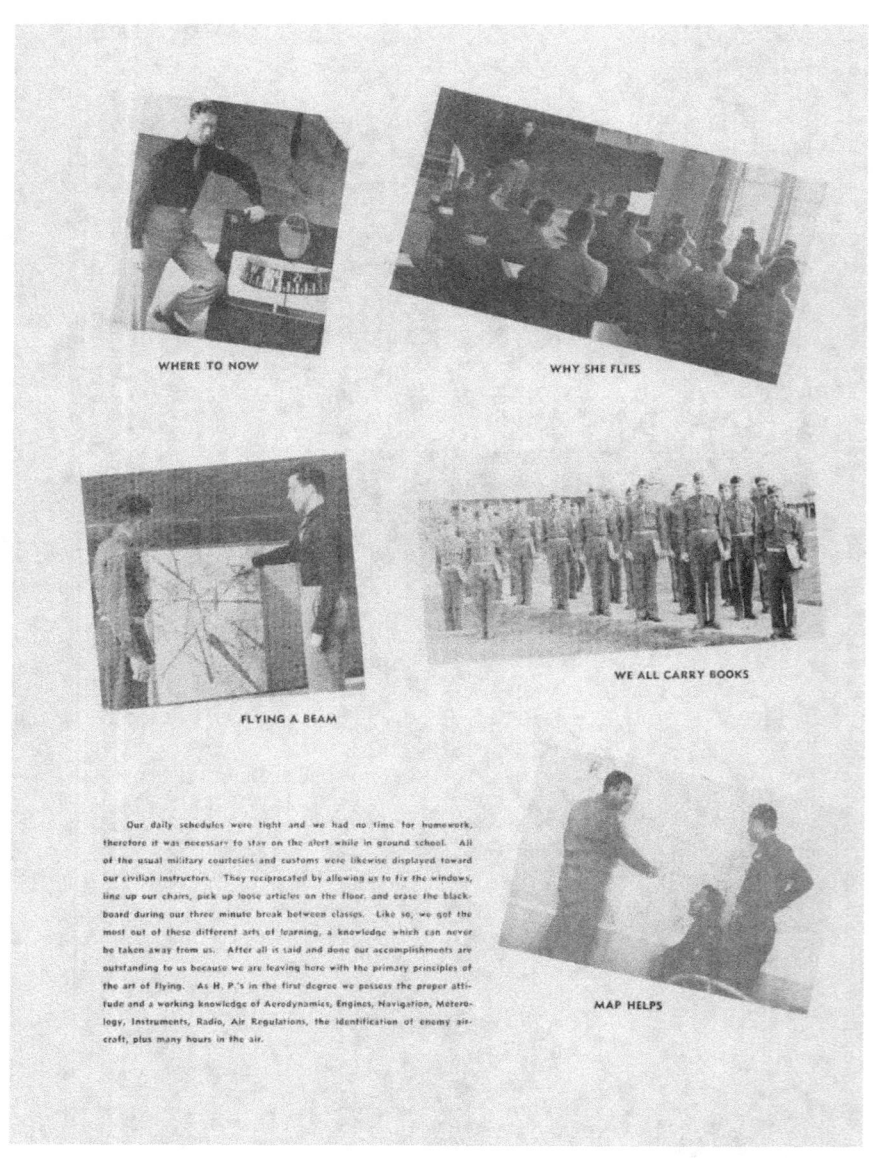

WHERE TO NOW

WHY SHE FLIES

FLYING A BEAM

WE ALL CARRY BOOKS

Our daily schedules were tight and we had no time for homework, therefore it was necessary to stay on the alert while in ground school. All of the usual military courtesies and customs were likewise displayed toward our civilian instructors. They reciprocated by allowing us to fix the windows, line up our chairs, pick up loose articles on the floor, and erase the blackboard during our three minute break between classes. Like so, we got the most out of these different arts of learning, a knowledge which can never be taken away from us. After all is said and done our accomplishments are outstanding to us because we are leaving here with the primary principles of the art of flying. As H. P.'s in the first degree we possess the proper attitude and a working knowledge of Aerodynamics, Engines, Navigation, Meteorology, Instruments, Radio, Air Regulations, the identification of enemy aircraft, plus many hours in the air.

MAP HELPS

Class 44-G annual
Thunderbird Field
Phoenix, Arizona
(continued)

Aviation Cadet Flying Suit
John H. Ingram Jr.

Aviation Cadet Uniform
John H. Ingram Jr.

Class 44-G annual
Thunderbird Field
Phoenix, Arizona

Jan 10, 1944

Hello Ma hello Pa,

Greetings from Paradise Valley, Arizona. Yep, that's where I am – in the middle of nowhere, but I like it. We left Santa Ana Thursday and the trip was fine. Had sleepers and ate in the dining car. The field is swell. We live in stucco huts, 10 men to a room and they are castles compared to the barracks we left behind. There are only about 4 or 5 hundred of us here so the place is small and convenient. Phoenix is the nearest town and I'll give you the lowdown on it when I get out next weekend.

I got my flying suit today and you should see me in them. I look like an Eskimo. I hope they'll keep me warm cause it really gets cold upstairs sometimes. We are flying Steermans and from what I've heard they are sweet ships. I'll let you know more about them when I take my first ride Monday.

We get 60 hours flying time here and a lot of it will be solo. I can't wait till Monday – and thank goodness the ground school isn't but two hrs a day.

I'll stop now until I get somewhere where it's quiet and I can write you a long letter. Here's where it counts folks and I am ready. Say a little prayer for me and don't worry. I'll be OK.

Love and Kisses,

J.H.

Jan 11, 1944

Hello Sis,

Got your letter today along with one from Mom and I'll just answer them both to you since I haven't written to you in ages.

Here I am at the great Thunderbird field and believe it or not, I kinda like it. We went out on the flight line for the first time today. My instructor is going to be a swell guy I think. The ships we are flying seem to be very stable and of course more powerful than the crates we flew in Texas. We'll be able to take pictures around here in a few weeks, so I'll send you all some of me in my flying suit and some of the ships we fly. I could talk all night about flying, so I'll just save it till I get home. Well, I have really covered the country since I left home and have seen just about everything. Out here we are located in a valley between two mountain ranges and it's really beautiful. Perfect flying weather too. I sure did hate to leave Hollywood though. I really had some big weekends there.

I sure would like to have been home for the dances this year, but like you said I guess they were pretty sloppy. I had a couple of letters from the gang and they didn't think much of them either. I still get a letter from Blondie almost once a month. Nice kid but not worth fighting for. Don't trust none of them. I would have liked to have seen Deedee. Ya know I had a crush on her last Xmas. I guess Pendergraph was home blowing his top. Call Mrs. Pendergraph and tell her to make Warren write to me.

Well, I've almost run out of news and besides the lights here are hard on my eyes, so I better sign off now. Write often will ya! and don't forget to say that little prayer for me.

Love and Kisses,

John H

Saturday

Hello Folks,

It's Sat. night here and I should be in town taking in a little civilization but we're still in quarantine so we'll just have to sack out this weekend (sleep through it). The quarantine ends next Wed. so I hope maybe I'll get a chance to go in next weekend. I've been flying every day this week and I don't think I'll ever get enough of it. For the last two days I seem to be really getting the feel of the ship and that's just what I want. Most of the boys seem to be getting pretty well chewed by the instructors, but mine seems to be full of patience. We had a good time up there today. I went up at 7:30 AM and believe me, it's cold up there early in the morning. We had spins and stalls today and we both got a kick out of it. We were up at 6000 ft. and he had me put it into a spin and then take my hand off the controls. I kicked her over in a spin and we both held our hands over our heads. We spun about five times and the ship came out of it and leveled off with neither one of us touching the controls. They are really wonderful ships and just as safe as an automobile. I wish I could get my hands on some pictures of this place. It's really a beautiful little place with a nice swimming pool included. If I graduate here I'll get a class annual like the one I got at Tech. Then you can see the place, the planes, me and my instructor.

Do you remember Shooky, the little blonde I dated when I was in Texas? Well, I got a letter from a friend of hers yesterday saying she got married. She married a 2nd Lt. (pilot). It seems to be a fad these days.

We have some student officers (8 of them) going through with us. They are commissioned officers learning to fly. One of them is a Capt. in the engineers and you should have seen him when he came down yesterday. He was pale as a ghost and he had puked all over the plane. I thought we would die laughing.

I can't think of nothing else much to say except that this is beautiful country. We are right down in the valley and every day I fly over the mountains and it's really a beautiful site. I think I better quit now and get to bed. I guess you wonder why I'm always talking about sleeping. You know you used to have to drive me to bed. Well next to flying now I love my sleep the best. Take care of yourselves, say a little prayer for me and write soon.

Love and Kisses,

JH.

I hope to solo in about another week. Wow, that's gonna be a great day. Me up there all by myself. I believe I could try it tomorrow if they'd let me. Would you believe this, It cost the government $20 an hour to teach me to fly. It's $7 million training and I can't let it slip through my fingers. The best there is and I'm getting it free. That's something worth digging in for. Good night.

Jan 17, 1944
Sunday

Hello Folks,

Just a line before I go to bed. We didn't get out this weekend so I've spent a very quiet day here on the base. A little bit too cool to go swimming, so I spent most of the day in the sack. I went to church services this morning. The chaplain is the best I've run into yet. Kinda old fellow and he can really drive things home.

Still haven't heard from you all since I got out here. Hurry up and write. I have a little more spare time here than I had back at Santa Ana so I do a little more writing than I did before.

I hope to be soloing after next week. That will be the day when I can take that plane up all by myself. Now don't you worry cause they certainly wouldn't send me up if they didn't think I could handle it. The ships are very stable and they fly better by themselves than they do with somebody at the controls. I wish you could see my instructor. He's the very image of old H.D. Leigh (remember) in looks and actions. I got a Xmas card from my old instructor back in Texas. I'll have to write to him.

Well I'll close now, take a shower, brush my teeth and go to bed. Keep praying for me and write soon.

Love and Kisses,

John H.

Don't forget to call the paper office and tell them to send my papers out here. They are the greatest kind of help to me.

January 22, 1944

Hello Folks,

I've been getting your letters OK and are they welcomed. (See about my papers). Well everything here is pretty well hunky-dory. My flying is about average I guess. Yesterday and the two days before I was (as us GI's say) pretty well pissed off. You know I told you that I had a swell instructor, well he's still tops but he has sure chewed my little twat for the last 3 days. The first six days were really sweet and I couldn't ask for better and then came Tuesday and he started chewing. Tuesday, Wednesday, and yesterday he did it but today he was as sweet as he could be. I had a good day today until the very last. I have been up doing spins and stalls and came back to the field. Flew the traffic pattern perfect, cut my throttle and came in for the landing, but I sat her down and didn't have the stick all the way back. He didn't say much but had me go in and write on the blackboard 50 times, "pull the damn stick back when landing," He came in later, looked at it and laughed. Tomorrow we shoot landings all day and I'll probably solo Monday or Tuesday, I can't wait!

Well, I get out tomorrow, our passes are from 6 o'clock tomorrow till 10 o'clock Sunday night. I'll let you know how this Phoenix layout is.

Got a letter from Aunt Ethel today. She sent me HGs address. She says uncle Harry weighs 220 pounds, wow. I think I'm gaining weight out here. I weighed about 150 when I left

Santa Anna. I got a package from grandmother. She seems to be in good health and happy. I can still read her writing. Dad says he didn't know the sailor boy who came to see you and Evelyn. I bet he does like to come out to the house. I sure do think a lot about Miss Matty, that's the little blonde (the one I dated in Texas) mother. I used to go out to their house on Sundays when I was in Texas. Always ate a big Sunday dinner with them and then take a good after dinner nap on the couch, just like at home.

I better slow up now and write HG. It's been ages since I wrote or heard from him. You all be sweet, take it easy and say a little prayer for me every night. I really love this flying and I just gotta make it. Keep your fingers crossed for me. Love and kisses. John H

Thanks for the stamps. I'll pay you the 25 bucks back this payday. We get paid in nine days.

— A spin, just to give you an idea, you cut the throttle, establish a normal glide, and start pulling the nose of the plane up to the stalling angle. When it stalls out and the stick is all the way back, kick full rudder and hang on. She flops over and starts spinning straight down. The ground is spinning like the devil too. To pull out of it, you kick full opposite rudder until she stops spinning, then dump the stick and pull out. Simple isn't it, but it's hard as heck to do.

January 23, 1944

Hello Folks,

Well, I am in ground school study hall tonight. I flunked a test on navigation the other day and I have to go to study hall every night. I don't know what happened to me on that test. I pulled my average up though and maybe I won't have to go next week.

I'm a little sad tonight. I was supposed to solo today and didn't get to. The guy that went up before me stayed all afternoon and when they finally did get down the afternoon was gone. I did get 14 minutes. We went up and shot two landings here on the home field. Two of the boys have check rides tomorrow which leaves the whole period for just two of us. I sure hope I get a chance tomorrow, more than likely I will.

I haven't heard from you all this week. I did get a paper today. You'll have to look into that paper business. That's the first one I've gotten in two weeks. They really help a lot and I look forward to getting them.

I guess everything at home is just like it is out here. Same old thing day in and day out. Looks like the end of the war will find me with my nose in a bunch of books and still getting chewed out by my instructors. So goes the life of an aviation cadet. Very discouraging at times but I'm just gonna keep on plugging and hope for the best.

Well, that's about all the news I know and that isn't much so I'll close now and study navigation for a while. I bet I could fly from here home with my eyes closed. They don't believe it though.

Be good, all of you. Let's all pray that I get out of this rut and write when you can.

Love and Kisses,

Johnny

January 25, 1944

Hello Folks,

I got two letters from you today. One was an old one that went through Santa Ana. Well we got a full day of sack time today. It rained here this morning believe it or not and we didn't fly. I'm supposed to solo tomorrow but since we didn't fly today it will probably be Wednesday before I get a crack at it by myself.

I went to town this weekend and I can't say much for the "burg". It's just an average city about the size of Durham. Just a typical western town with cowboys and Indians making up the majority of the people. Nothing much to do. They have a 1 o'clock curfew which messes up everything. We got in kind of late and couldn't find a place to stay. We finally found a guy who sent us out to a private home. It was an old lady who had three sons in the service and she sure was nice to us. We slept in rooms over the garage like the one Aunt Ethel has. She gave us breakfast the next morning and we just made ourselves at home for a while. She wants us to come back and I guess we will unless we can get a hotel room reserved.

I tried to call you on Sunday but she told me there would be a five hour delay so I canceled the call. I'll try again soon. I am going to have some pictures made soon and this time it's on the level. I got a letter from Gordon Whitted today and he is still waiting for an opening at preflight. I also got one from my buddy who was held over back in Santa Ana. He's a mess and so was his letter. They just informed us that we would have a stand by inspection in an hour. They can't stand to see us rest for a little while. I better quit now and do a little brushing up.

Take it easy and keep those letters rolling in. Tell everybody hello for me and keep those fingers crossed.

Love,

JH

January 28, 1944

Hello Folks,

I haven't got much time, but I got to give you the good news. I finally soloed! Yep, I took her up all by myself today. We went over to the auxiliary field today and I had shot about eight landings then my instructor got out of the ship. He said he didn't have his insurance paid up and he was scared to ride with me and for me to go up by myself. He tried to look serious but all the time he was halfway smiling.

Well, I've never had a better feeling in all my life as I did when I taxied out to take off. I felt about like I did the night dad let me have the car (it was new then) to take the little Buchanan gal to the big dance. Well I got set for the takeoff and the front cockpit had never looked as big as it did right then. I made a good takeoff and a few seconds later there I was all by myself and nobody to rave at me if I did something wrong. I never did have the least bit of fear because I knew before I started that I could do it. Well I flew the traffic pattern and came in for my landing. I had to give it a little throttle to get over the fence but I got over it and set her down as gently as I could. Boy I really felt like letting out a yell and all the way back to the stage house I revved up the engine, about like double clutching a car. He was waiting for me and he looked at me and smiled, said I made a pretty low turn on the base leg approach but it was OK. We didn't have time for everyone but if I can stay on the ball and pass a couple of check rides next week I'll be checking ships out by myself and getting in two or three hours a day.

That's it folks. Keep praying for me and I'll keep on plugging. This is really what I want more than anything I know of.

Keep those fingers crossed, love and kisses,

your son, John H.

February 2, 1944

Hello Folks,

I'm still in study hall, passed the last test but it wasn't high enough to pull up my average. I think we got another one coming up this week and I'll really hit that one and bring up my average.

Your son has now about one hour by his lonesome self in the Stearman. I had my second supervised solo yesterday. Shot six landings and stayed up for 35 minutes. I think I can fly much better by myself than I can with him in there. Seems like when he's with me I am in a strain for fear he'll ball me out for some little something and when I am by myself I'm much more relaxed and I can keep my mind on the ship. We had two little accidents this week but nobody got hurt. Yesterday, two B.T.'s ran together. Messed up the planes a little. Today some guy slapped on his brakes too quickly and he nosed over on his back. Nobody was hurt, just scared a little.

I went into Phoenix last week and met a nice girl. She goes to high school there and her name is Julie. Good looking and the best dancer in town. She is lots of fun and I enjoy being with her. Lots better than standing on the street corner or waiting out a theater line.

I'm looking forward to taking pictures. Next week will be upperclassman and we can take pictures. We are all set and as soon as they give the word, I'll have all kinds of pictures of this place for you.

Well, I'll sign off now and write again tomorrow night. Say a little prayer for me and take care of yourselves, Love and kisses,

John Herbert Jr.

February 4, 1944

Hello Folks,

Got your letter today answering the sad one I wrote. I didn't know I was feeling that low that night. Just kinda looked over my letters like that, I write just like I feel anyway.

Things here are pretty well on the up and up. We are on the flightline five hours now and it's all work and no play. I'm checking planes out now. I get so much duel time and so much solo time every day. I was up early this morning by myself practicing some new maneuvers. Had a big time zooming around. I've got about 16 hours in now, and now that we are on the five hour shift, I'll be piling them up.

The upperclassmen are finishing up here this week and will probably ship out for basic next week. Then we will be the old timers of this place. Seems like it was no time since I've staggered in this place all google eyed over the planes and wondering if I could fly or not.

I sure did laugh about LaMarr saying his prayers. Tell him I don't think there is any danger of them sending me home on account of my legs. Mom, I'm getting your letters OK now and the papers too, so don't you worry.

I've got about $200 saved in my pocket and I don't know what to do with it, (we got paid the other day). I'll just send part of it home and you can buy bonds or do what you want with it. I have blown all I could and can't get rid of it. If I was back in Hollywood it would be a different story.

Well, I'll close now and hit the sack. I've never been this tired since I've been here. I didn't realize flying was so tiresome. Say a little prayer for me and keep your fingers crossed, love and kisses,

Johnny

February 8, 1944

Hello Folks,

I'm not in study hall tonight. Made 100 on my navigation test today and pulled up my average. Don't laugh, but I am in the latrine now. I can write better in here where it's quiet. We fly (in my mind) 24 hours a day. At night everybody sits around and gives a detailed account of what they did and I am always right in the middle of it so when I write I have to find a secluded spot.

We had a little fun this morning. We were at the flight line early. I got my ship, warmed her up, and taxied down to take off. There was a fog rolling in from the south and the weather was closing in fast. As I taxied down I kept wondering if they were going to let us take off in that soup solo. Well I got down, checked my instruments and engine and was waiting to take off. The weather kept closing in and I kept my eyes on the control tower expecting to get the red light (which means don't take off) any minute. It never did come so I headed into the wind and started to take off when I glanced up at the hangers and the guys were jumping up and down waving their handkerchiefs and about that time the red flag went up in the smoke pots were lit. That means the field is closed and those who were up return immediately. I taxied back, parked on the line, got out and we all had fun watching the guys trying to make the field in the fog. they had to send instructors up in BT's to find some of them who were roaming around up over the overcast and didn't see the smoke signal. It's really lots of fun. We get a kick out of every new thing that happens to us. I wish I could have got off the ground for the excitement this morning. I'm beginning to feel like a veteran in the air now. Me at the controls of a $28,000 airplane. Makes you kinda look up to yourself and think it's too good a deal to pass up.

Well folks, I promised you this for 8 months now and this time it's on the level. I have an appointment with the photographer next Saturday. If nothing happens I'll have a picture for you soon. The reason I've been slow on it is this: most studios, since business is so good now, just throw any old kind of work on a soldier and get away with it. This place I'm going to is OK. I was out at the ladies house last Saturday night and Sunday. I was down at her studio and saw her work and it's strictly class. We have pictures taken of us today with our planes and instructors. I ordered six of them so when I get them I'll send you some. Got a letter from HG today, he says he's been transferred to the engineers. He's in a real man's outfit now and I know he'll like it. That cooking business he was in before is a soft job and it's kinda looked down on by the men. He'll go places and see things now. Also heard from Totsy. I really enjoy her letters. Most of them that write, I can kind of read between the lines and see that it bores them to write but she spills everything and seems like she enjoys it. I sat here and wrote 4 pages and for once they made a little sense. I got to write HG. He sent me some pictures he had taken Xmas and he really is getting fat as a hog. The engineers will take that off. Just give them time. I'll sign off now. Tell God to make me a good pilot as LaMarr says and keep your fingers crossed.

Love and kisses,
Johnny

February 14, 1944

Hello Folks,

Well, I'm back from a pretty fair weekend. Dated Julie last night. We went dancing and stuff. I finally got my pictures taken for you. I've been dreading getting them taken because I had to lug the flying togs in town and back but this week three of us packed the stuff in a suitcase and so it's all over now. I sure hope they turn out all right. I had four settings taken. Two in the flying stuff and two in my uniform. I'll see the proofs next Saturday and maybe next week they'll be ready.

Got a phone call this evening and it was old Jimmy Knight. Remember my buddy that's a brother of Mrs. Ezzle. Ya know I left him back in S.A. He's out here now at Thunderbird #1 a few miles from here. I'll meet him in Phoenix next week. He's a mess. Crazy as they come.

The flying is coming along OK I guess. I got around 30 hours now. Since we've been flying five hours a day now I am so tired at night I can hardly move. We started aerobatics and they are fun, loops, rolls, etc. We got cross country down to Maricopa to Three Points and back this week. That will be fun.

I guess that's about all I know for now. I'll write again soon. You all do the same. Take it easy, say that little prayer and keep those fingers crossed for me.

Love and Kisses,
J.H.

February 17, 1944

Hello Folks,

Must be a busy week for you at home. I haven't heard from you since Saturday. Got a few papers is all.

Things here are practically the same. Something new and flying every day. I had a check ride today. Passed that one but still got an army check coming up. The one today was a little on the humorous side. I rode with Mr. Groomer (check pilot) and he didn't have his teeth in. Every time he told me to do a maneuver over the earphones it was nothing but a bunch of blah blah jumbled up words and I couldn't understand a thing he said. I gave him a pretty good ride though and he passed me. I hope I can come through on the army check. We got cross country down to Maricopa and back tomorrow. Fly it duel first and then solo. It's a nice trip. About 120 miles. Some beautiful country too. I'm still working on aerobatics, loops, rolls, spins, etc. I come out in some crazy positions sometimes but that helps you to find the mistakes you make.

I'm keeping my fingers crossed for this weekend. Somehow I managed to collect a few gigs this week and one or two more will keep me in this weekend. We got a pretty rugged inspection coming off tomorrow. If I can just get by that I'll make it. I want to get in this week to see my picture proofs.

Well, I better quit now and hit the sack. I've got link trainers tomorrow morning at 6:50. You know the little instrument ship with the hood that never gets off the ground. Be good, write soon and keep those fingers crossed for me.

Love and Kisses,

Johnny

February 21, 1944

Hello Folks,

Just got in from another weekend in Phoenix. About the same this week. I dated Julie last night and we took in a movie this afternoon. The first picture I've seen in a long time. I very seldom go to the show. The few hours we get off are too valuable to waste in a theater.

Well, I saw my proofs yesterday and they are not so bad. The ones I had taken in my flying dogs are not what I'd like to have had. She said I'd get the finished product in two weeks. I was satisfied with them. They look just like me. Oh! Yeah! I got your letter and pictures yesterday and the pictures are fine. I never thought of this guy Scotty being such a big hunk of a man. He looks OK to me. I don't know whether he knows it or not but he's got the best set up right now he'll ever get. I had the same thing at Texas Tech, and boy what a life. Live in college dorms, good food, etc. You never realize just how nice a deal it was until you get out of it.

Well, did I tell you that I passed my army check last week and what a relief it was. I was checked by Lt. Fraizier and he was in a crabby mood that day and I sure did sweat that ride out. It seems that he didn't like the way I recovered from an accidental stall and also I glided too fast on the approach leg of the traffic pattern so I got chewed thoroughly for that. He flunked one of our boys and our instructor didn't like it a bit. I really have a huge time up there now. I can do a pretty fair snap roll, half roll, and slow roll now.

As soon as I get used to being on my back (upside down) I'll get those down pat. I'm gradually learning that little ship, just what it will do and what it won't do. I sure do get in some of the darndest predicaments finding that out. You know we haven't got but three more weeks here. The nine weeks sure have gone fast.

Heck! I have run out of news already. I can never write all I want to. I can think of lots to tell you until I start to write. I guess I'll go now. Be good, all of you. Say that little prayer for me and write soon, love and kisses,

John H

Evelyn sure has grown up to be a good looking girl. It didn't surprise me at all.

February 24, 1944

Hello Folks,

Most of the guys went over to the recreation hall tonight to see a movie and it's so quiet and peaceful here in the barracks. I'll hurry and write you a line before they get back and start raising a racket.

A front moved in on us from the coast yesterday and the weather has been bad for the past two days but from the looks of the sky tonight it'll clear up tomorrow. You see I've been studying weather ever since the first day in preflight and believe it or not I know quite a lot about what's happening and what's going to happen. You didn't know that, did you? It seems kind of funny to me, nine months ago the sky was just something that was over your head to me and now I can tell you everything that's going on up there. I read weather maps and coded station reports. You see, weather is very important to you when you fly. Yep, I learn things every day, it's really surprising.

They are still rushing us. It was supposed to be a 9 weeks schedule here but they put us on a 8 weeks schedule and we are to finish up by Saturday week. Our graduation dance is Saturday night the 3rd and I guess we'll ship out the 4th. I hope I can stay on the ball and get out of here OK. I have two more check rides coming up. The least little thing can finish you. I've got 45 hours now, 20 duel and 25 solo. I took my cross-country duel the other day and it was really fun. My instructor was the pilot and I was the navigator. So I sit back with my maps and charts and computers and stuff. I figure the course including wind correction, deviation, variation, etc. Hit it right on the nose too. Didn't have a bit of trouble. He really had a big time trying to ball me up and he almost did several times. I guess I'll fly it solo about Friday or Saturday.

Well, I want to ask you a favor. I am in need of a shoe ration stamp if you can possibly spare one. I bought a pair right after I got in and they're really all shot now. I don't know how they dish out those stamps for this year but if you can spare one I would appreciate it. I kinda hate to go to our graduation dance in the G.I. clodknockers. Don't let me put any of you out of anything though.

The boys are back from the show and the place has suddenly turned into a madhouse so I guess I better close for now. We have to fall out in a little while anyway to sign the payroll. Be good and take things easy. Write soon and don't forget that little prayer for me.

Good night all, love and kisses,

JH

February 29, 1944

Hello Folks,

I just got time for a short note. We're trying to make up the time we lost last week due to the weather and they're pushing us every minute of the day so I better turn in early tonight to be able to make it tomorrow.

Well, I had my last two check rides yesterday and today and passed them both. I sure do feel good about it. My instructor seemed pretty happy about it too. If I just stay on the ball and sweat out this last week I'll be OK.

I gotta cut this now. They just announced " lights out in 10 minutes" and I got to fix my bed. I'm sending you a little paper that we put out here once a week and maybe it will be of some interest to you.

Say that little prayer for me and write soon,

Love and Kisses,

J.H.

March 3, 1944

Hi Everybody,

Got your letter today with the shoe stamp and it was a lifesaver, thanks a million. Since last Sunday we had perfect flying weather, but today another storm blew in from the coast and things don't look so good for us. We are supposed to be through by Saturday, but I don't see how we will do it.

Well, I came through on all my checks and it's just a matter of eight more hours in the air now. We have been flying 6 1/2 hours a day all week and I just fall in bed every night completely worn out. It's really work to be kicking those planes around up there. I went on another solo cross-country the other day and almost went to sleep at the stick. My tail was plum numb from it.

It's hard to believe but eight weeks ago it was just a dream and now I am a pretty fair pilot. Can do almost anything in the books too. It's really the life.

I had a letter from Jr. Henson today. I wrote him last week. He gripes about school and I gripe about the army.

I ought to have plenty of pictures to send to you next week. I get the big ones Saturday and I've got some others of the planes that me and my instructor ordered. My buddy and I have two rolls of film we're going to take when everything slacks up and we have time.

I hope all of you are fine. I have never felt better in my life and feel a bit old but I don't act that way. The guys can vouch for that. It doesn't make me feel any good though when the girls in town guess my age anywhere from 22 to 25. You can draw your own conclusions from the pictures.

I guess this is all for tonight. Write soon and say that little prayer.

Love,

J

March 8, 1944

Hello Folks,

It seems like ages since I wrote to you. I've really been busy trying to get out of this place OK. I don't like to write you anything unless it's definite so I can tell you now that everything is OK. I finished ground school with an 83 average and could have done better but I never studied. I finished my flying up too, with 65 hours and 03 minutes. I was out on the flight line this evening and believe it or not it made me feel a little sad to see those little old crates taking off and know that I've taken my last ride in them. It just didn't seem natural not climbing into one of them.

I'm one step up the ladder and believe me it's a long ladder. I feel now about basic just like I felt about primary. It's going to be tough and I better keep digging. They say after you get by primary there is nothing to worry about but the more I fly the less I find that I know about it. You gotta know everything. As Dad used to tell me, "I can always learn."

I've tried to call you all for the last 4 days but I just can't hit it lucky enough to get through. We had our dance last Saturday night and it was fine. Everything came off swell. I met Jimmy Knight in town too, and it was swell to be with him again.

Did you get the pictures? I hope you like them. The one in the togs doesn't look like me. You can send the extras to whomever you think would appreciate them. I got a nice letter from Betty Peak. I'll have to answer it.

Well, I'll ship out this weekend. I doubt if I will go far. I signed up for fighter pilot and those that want to be fighter pilots usually go to Marana, which is just 150 miles from here, near Tucson. I'll lay my bottom dollar that I will go there. I'll probably finish at Luke Field, which is just 50 miles from here. Just 18 more weeks. It hardly seems possible.

We get our class books Saturday and also I'll get some pictures that we took here. The book will show you the whole layout here. I'll send you all of them.

I'm getting tired and sleepy now so I better hit the sack and get all the rest I can. I'll be on the go again next week and it will be 9 long hard weeks before I get another rest like this.

I hope all of you are fine. Don't worry about me, I am OK and ready for anything they throw at me. Keep praying for me and writing as often as you can.

Good night, love and kisses,

J.H.

March 13, 1944

Hello Folks,

This is just a short note to tell you that I'm shipping out here tonight. We've been out on pass since last Thursday at noon and I didn't have time to write.

They read us the shipping orders last night and me and a bunch of us are going back to California. I thought for sure I was going to Marana, which is only 150 miles south of here but it looks like I'm going to Ontario California, only 35 miles from LA in Hollywood. It sounds like a swell deal and if it is I don't see how I got in on it.

Maybe I'll be able to see some of my old buddies back in California. We got our class books and pictures. I'll get them off to you as soon as I can. You'll like the book, it will answer all of your questions.

Well, I'm kind of glad I'm leaving this desert and going back to civilization again. I sure enjoyed it out here though. We've all had a grand time. I'm looking forward to better days.

This is a pretty big step. We are really getting into the airplanes now, bigger, heavier, more powerful, and faster. I can't wait!

Well folks, California here I come, right back where I started from. Say a little prayer for me and write too.

John H. at Ontario, California

a/c John H. Ingram

Class of 44 G

2nd AAFFTD

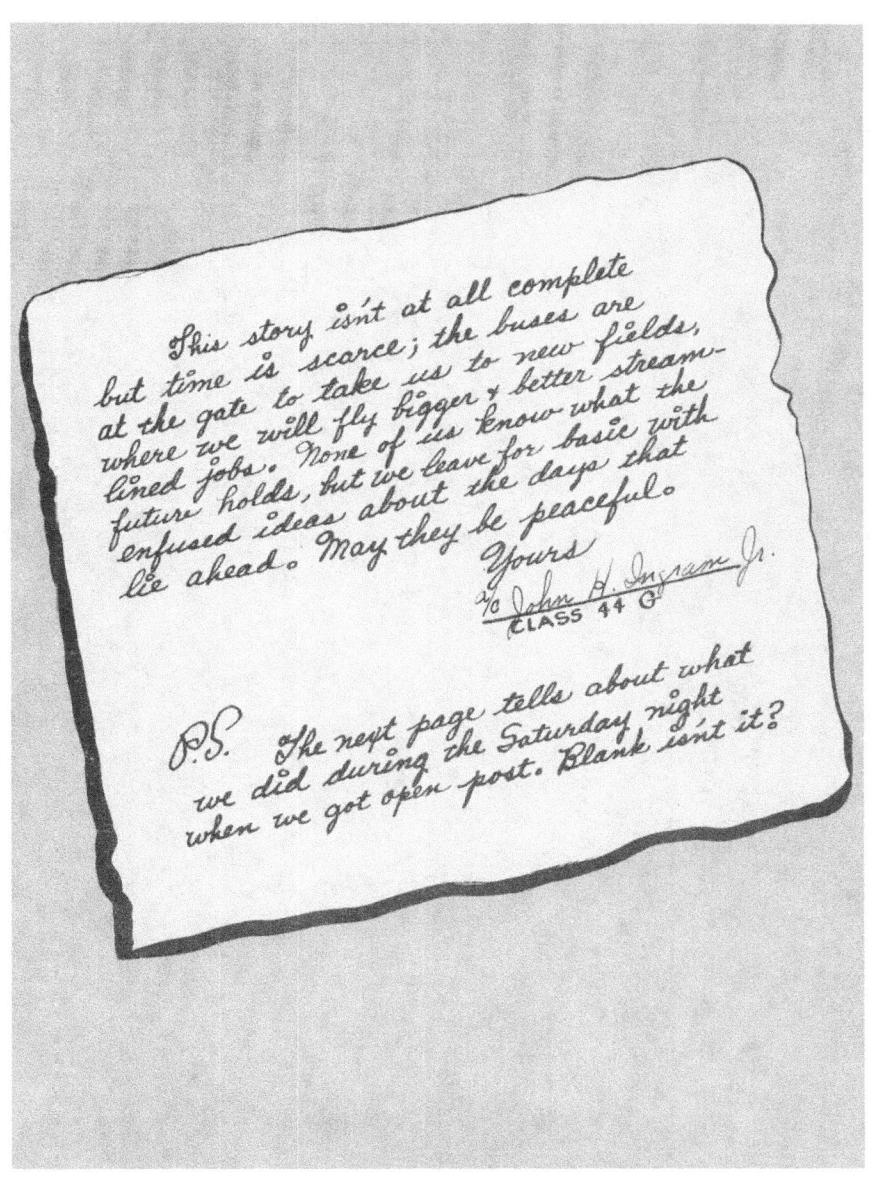

This story isn't at all complete
but time is scarce; the buses are
at the gate to take us to new fields,
where we will fly bigger & better stream-
lined jobs. None of us know what the
future holds, but we leave for basic with
enfused ideas about the days that
lie ahead. May they be peaceful.

Yours

a/c John H. Ingram Jr.
CLASS 44 G

P.S. The next page tells about what
we did during the Saturday night
when we got open post. Blank isn't it?

Class 44-G annual
Thunderbird Field
Phoenix, Arizona

MARCH 13 - MAY 9, 1944

ONTARIO, CA
BASIC TRAINING

"This is the BT-15, the ship I'll be flying"

Squadron NO. 3, Class 44-G, March 21, 1944

"This is the control tower and the plane I'm flying — Getting in the big time now!"

"This is a picture of the barracks. Can't see much but they are really nice!"

Instructor: R. E. Daniels; R. J. Tapscott, R. E. Bush,
J. H. Ingram, Jr., kneeling, J. R. Lienau.

Photo of his flying buddies and his instructor in his annual from the base

Squadron Three - One Step Nearer the Goal

We have included in Squadron Three, such famous personages as "Hey' you people" Martin, "Give me a bearing to Cal-Aero" Allavie, "Donald Duck" Leneau, Clay Pidgeon, Red Falcon, Black Dog, The Crimson Ace, "Davis Wing" Dixon, "Eek" Maggs, "Yuh got anything to eat" Mackley, "Get out-o-hea" Zakian, "Up and Down" Hillburn, "Buddy" Romekema, "Fearless" Fausett, "It Sure feels better" Sorenson, and many others that make up the roster.

The squadron started in the usual manner. Upon their arrival at the "Institute" they were greeted by a very sharp reception committee. After being assigned to quarters they were taught the niceties of barracks care. The second lesson included mess hall sprinting, and extracting instructors teeth from parachutes. After these prelim-

inaries they were introduced to the more difficult tasks. Instruments, night flying and formation flying. Ground school was a snap with simple terms to learn like the modulated gamma-ray antenas who's skip distance and topographic range oscillates external factors, keeping volume constant and prosines R-K-IMI, whose caloric variation deviate Buy Ballots Law of coriolis gradients. Furthermore the adiabatic insulation radiating occlusions dissipate the MPs-MPWs and MPKs. Now if an MPW meets a CPK what have you got? You can always blame it on a temperature inversion.

After completing basic training, the men in Squadron Three will be one step closer to their desired goal. That goal is to become better and more efficient exterminators of the enemies of the free and happy way of our lives.

His Squadron

March 13, 1944

Hello Folks,

I'm back here in sunny California just 45 minutes from LA. I am in Ontario, California.

Just got in today but so far it looks like a swell deal. I hope and pray it will be. Looks like I'm hitting all the famous places. This place here is supposed to be one of the best. It has a big name anyway. The best living conditions I've ever seen. We have two men to a room with a bath and the chow is fine.

We start flying in a couple of days and I can hardly wait for that. It's going to be tough and I have to keep plugging. I'm getting on up the old latter, it seems.

I hope all of you are well and happy. I sure wish I could see you. Looks like I get further away from home every day. I was hoping I'd get a little nearer to home so you all could come to see me on Easter but I'm so far now I guess I'll just have to wait till I get through.

Well, I got to get on the ball now to sweat out this basic. Just keep praying for me and I'll give it all I got. Just gotta make it. Hurry and write, I'm thinking of you all the time.

Love and kisses,

J———-

March 17, 1944

Hello everybody,

First thing I'd better tell you is that for a while here I'm not going to be able to write to you very much. We are on the tightest schedule I've ever heard or seen. I am up at 5:30 AM and go like fighting fire till 8:30 at night, boy are we griping. All of us are plenty fed up with it already. Sometimes I wonder just what keeps me going at this grind. The flying is wonderful but the ground school is nuts along with PT and drill. I should have had a couple years of college before I ever attempted acting like this. I figure if those guys can do it I can. I'll have to do more studying than they do though.

Well, I got two hours and five minutes in the BT's now and my instructor is really tops. So far we've been getting along fine but I won't be surprised when he does start chewing my can. I hope to be able to solo out by Monday. That is if I can get that procedure down pat. Boy, you really work every minute in these ships. The Stearman back in primary had only a few instruments and gadgets, but this thing has thousands and you're constantly checking and working with them. It's like jumping from a T model Ford to a big Cadillac.

Well they have really got us all in a dump as I told you before. We were supposed to get out this weekend but some guy came down with the scarlet fever and now we are restricted and confined to the post. There's nothing more demoralizing than that. I'll be so fogged out by Sunday because I want to go out.

Folks, I'm going to do all I can to get you out to this place for one thing because our graduation day from here will really be something worth seeing. I wish you all could come out. We're going to have a big ceremony along with a big air show and I'm hoping and praying that I'll be able to be in it. There will be formation flying, aerobatics, and all that stuff. They tell us it's going to be a pretty big event. You could really see me doing some flying.

I just wrote to Betty Jean Price. Did I tell you that I got a nice letter from her? I got a telegram today and as usual it like to scared me to death. They always do. It was from one of my buddies over at Oxnard. He wanted me to meet him this weekend in Hollywood.

Well I'd better quit now and get to bed. Tomorrow's a long day with 40 million things to do. Hurry and write, it's been a long time since I've heard from you. Say a little prayer for me and let's all keep our fingers crossed. Just 16 more weeks and the great day will come.

Love and kisses,

J.H.

March 20, 1944

Hello Mom,

Hi, I wrote you a letter last night but after reading it over a couple of times this morning I decided not to send that one and write you another.

Some guy came down with the scarlet fever and they restricted us this weekend and the letter I wrote last night was just one gripe after another.

Well folks, I've soloed the BT now and with only 3 1/2 hours duel. I got 50 minutes of solo time in yesterday. Boy, I really felt like a hot pilot in that big baby with the canopy open and an earphone set on. I got a prince of an instructor and he really knows his stuff.

I got a letter from you the other day. I guess it was the last one you wrote to Thunderbird. You said Mildred was up for a few days. I'll be looking for some letters from you this week. I hope you've got my new address by now.

Mom, I bought you a pair of silver wings today and will send them as soon as possible. They are pilot wings but after all, I'm a pretty fair one and I may be a good one someday. I want you to wear them all the time.

Hope you got the pictures by now. Also sent you the book the other day. Well I guess that's about all the news I have for you today. I think I will go back to bed and catch up on all that sleep I lost this past week. Boy they really keep us stepping around here. We are on the go from 5:30 AM till 8:00 PM for 6+7 days a week. Say that little prayer for me and write soon.

Love and kisses,

J————

March 22, 1944

Hello folks,

I got your letter and pictures today and I'm glad now that you know where I am. I still can't understand why you haven't got the big pictures and the book. Maybe they'll be there in a few days. The pictures were fine. LaMarr sure has grown and Dad really looks good. Mom, you will always be the same.

Well, we're kind of getting into the swing of things around here. It's been tough but as soon as we get used to it, it won't be so bad. The ground school is going to be tough. Boy, if I ever get through this I'll really have something.

The flying is coming along pretty good so far. I haven't got any more solo time since last Saturday, but I hope I'll be able to check a ship out before the week is gone.

So, ole Mutt is home on furlough. He wrote to me that he had one coming up. I guess I'll spend my weekend in LA and Hollywood. It's OK, but it takes more money. Back in Phoenix I could have the biggest kind of time on five bucks.

You should see me. You know they have made us keep our head shaved just about everywhere we've been. Here they are a little lax on it and I've apparently got a little hair on my head. It looks so good I stand and comb it all the time. If I ever get those wings and bars I'm going to let it grow down to my crotch. Ha!

That's all for tonight folks. I gotta hit the sack so I will last through tomorrow. Stick with me.

Love and kisses,

J——-

March 25, 1944

Hello Folks,

For the past two days I've gotten two or three letters from you and enjoyed everyone. I'm glad the pictures and the book came through OK. The book covers primary pretty thoroughly.

The quarantine is lifted and we get out tomorrow night to kinda stretch our legs. I'm going to try to meet some of my buddies that I was with at Santa Ana in L.A. It will be good to shoot the bull with them again.

Well, things here are going pretty well so far. I made some good grades in ground school this week. I hope I can keep that up. Been doing a little solo flying this week. Today I took a sectional map with me and just rode around and looked at the country. It was really interesting. This is beautiful country out here and in this section particularly there are a lot of things to see. I was up over Baldy Peak, 10,000 feet, and it was all covered with snow. Then on top of one mountain I found the Mount Wilson Observatory. The largest telescope in the world is there. They study the stars through it. Got up high enough so I could see Catalina island. Shucks, there were so many things I couldn't begin to name them all.

My instructor is still the best. Tell you the truth, that's the first guy I've ever run into that I could fly better with him in the rear cockpit than I can by myself.

Nope, I don't get my wings here. Truthfully I still have a good ways to go but if nothing happens, and I hope not, I'll graduate in the latter part of June. You see I still got nine weeks of advanced after this. Let's all keep our fingers crossed and I'll do my best. I will close now for tonight, but keep praying and write soon.

Love and kisses,

J

March 28, 1944

Hello Folks,

I just got back from the big town and I'm still fogged. I am always griping about getting a weekend off for a little rest and relaxation and I am my son of a gun if I am twice as tired after a weekend off than I am after a whole week on the base.

My instructor took us in this week. He's really a good Joe. We took in all the old places we used to go when we were back in Santa Ana. Hollywood is still stark raving mad. This morning we were standing on a corner there in LA right after breakfast and some guy walked up and grabbed me by the arm and it was Steve Killebrew. Do you remember him? The guy I went to Richmond Virginia with a couple of times. He's in the Marines and he is stationed down here at Oceanside. We were both surprised as the devil to see each other. His folks are still living in Texas.

How do you like my new pen? I got tired of struggling along with these $.98 goose feathers, so today I up and purchased myself a $21 Eversharp, guaranteed forever, pen and pencil set. It's a beautiful set, maroon and gold.

How are things around the house today? Same as usual I guess. Went to church this morning. I haven't gotten a paper since I left Thunderbird, so if you have time, how about looking into that for me, will you? For all I know the war may be over by now.

I'm still studying my tail off and trying to learn how to fly the army way. I had a solo ship yesterday for two hours but the visibility wasn't so good around here and so I sat in the ready all evening waiting for the haze to lift so I could fly and it never did. I hope I can still get those two hours tomorrow.

Well folks, I better quit now. I don't want to break in my pin too fast. Let's all keep our fingers crossed, and don't forget a little prayer for me. Write soon

Love and kisses,

J———-

April 1, 1944

Hello Folks,

Got a couple of letters from you today and yesterday. Keep'em rolling if you can, also see about my papers too.

Well, this week sure has flown by, here it is Friday and tomorrow we can see the big lights again. It's been a good week all around for us. Today was payday and that always livens things up. Got a letter from HG yesterday. Says he hasn't been home in a month but he's planning on going soon. Also Mutt wrote and told me all about his few days at home. He's getting a 10 day delay in route in two weeks. The lucky son of a gun.

I was up with the squadron commander today. I rode with him last Monday and didn't do so hot, felt bad. Today he said I really gave him a good ride, far more superior to the one last Monday and that made me feel good. We are getting right up in the hours now and will probably start night flying and formation flying soon.

Yep! I got your mail and everything is alright. I guess you got mine ok too. This stamp business is a mess now isn't it?

Folks, I believe you are rushing me a bit, so is everybody else. It does seem like I should be graduating, I've been in so long, but that day still looks a long way off to me. There's a thousand and one things to learn in order to be a good combat pilot and you can't rush them.

Oh my gosh! It's 9:25 already and we got this floor to wax for tomorrow's inspection so I better close now and get on it.

Take it easy all of you and keep writing. I'll try to squeeze in a few more letters per week. Let's all keep praying, and I'll do my best.

Love and kisses,

Johnny

April 5, 1944

Hello folks,

I haven't had very much time to myself here lately and here I am stacked up with letters to answer. Everybody waits so long and then it looks like they all write at once. I have been getting your letters OK and the papers are coming in now too. Well I had a pretty good weekend this past week. The girls over at Pomona College invited some of us over to a dance Saturday night and we had a huge time. Of course we all took a chance on drawing for dates and some of us didn't do so bad. The place was really ritzy, everything formal. There were a few taxpayers (civilians) there in tux. That made me a little homesick.

Everything here is about as good as it could be, I guess. Can you believe it? We are upperclassmen next week. Time flies. Start instrument and night flying too, oh me! We got a 200 mile cross country coming up one day this week. I've been working on mine for the last two days. Plotting courses, checking weather reports, timing checkpoints, you know, all of the maps and chart work. All of that is done before you start out. Me and my buddies here that flew together back at Thunderbird had a letter from our old instructor back there, G. Pallas. He was a mess. Says he has never had one of his boys to wash out in basic and we better stay on the ball.

How is everybody there? I guess LaMarr and the witch hazel bottle are getting a little duel time now, (vaccination). Well I better quit now and do a little studying. Test tomorrow in radio communication. Be swell all of you and let's keep praying and smiling.

Love and kisses

J———-

April 11, 1944

Hello folks,

I hope you had a nice Easter Sunday. It hasn't seemed much like Easter to me. Maybe it was because I couldn't be with you all at church this morning. I hope you liked the roses. I had corsages in mind but I thought maybe they would be too late getting there.

They let us out last Friday night so we had a nice long weekend. An order has come down that we fly only five days a week now so it looks possible that we may be getting Saturday and Sunday off from now on. I sure hope so.

We started out to spend a quiet weekend on the base. Got to Long Beach and got settled but Saturday it turned cool so we didn't do any beachcombing. I did go shopping and I bought myself an Easter outfit. Pair of sun-tans. We go into them next week.

Well tomorrow we are upperclassmen. Start instrument, night, and formation flying too. Another case where you've either got it or not. I sure hope I have it. I got a big cross country coming up in the morning too so I better hit the sack early tonight. Take it easy all of you and write when you can. Keep praying and I'll do my best.

Love and kisses

J———-

April 13, 1944

Hello Dad,

Got your letter a little while ago and it sure was good to hear from you again. You know that's the first I've heard from you since Christmas. Well this has been a swell week for us guys. We had open post last night and we get off again in a couple of hours, plus the weekend. If it keeps up like this my money won't hold out. This comes once in a blue moon though. See, the upper class graduates today and graduation week is always a pretty big affair. The exercises come off at 2 o'clock with a big air show and all the trimmings. Of course we'll be in there too. I hope I'll see this day come for me.

We start instrument, night, and formation flying next week. Got to stay on the ball. Well, how is the plumbing business? Still the same old grind I guess. When I graduate, I hope, I want you to take a long vacation, come out here and see some of this country. A bunch of us are going up to Big Bear this weekend. Pretty ritzy joint. It's up on Mt. Baldy. Plenty of ice-skating and skiing. We've done just about everything else so we decided we would take a shot at that.

Pop, I better close now and get ready for chow. Take it easy old man and write again when you find time. Tell everybody hello for me and I'm thinking of them.

Love,
John Herbert Jr.
-keep your fingers crossed-

April 18, 1944

Hello folks,

Well, I haven't been still long enough for the past five days to sit down and write you a line. We've been off the post more than we've been on, but it's all over now and it's back to the old grind. I'm a little down and out tonight. They split up our squadron today and half of the boys stayed on night and instrument flying while half of us are working on transition and formation flying. I am in the latter half and somehow I am a little disappointed. Then again I think it's for the best. This will only last for two weeks then we trade places and we get the rest of our instrument and night work while they get transition and formation. Let's keep on hoping and praying because I just gotta make it!

I've been having a little trouble this past week. One of my back teeth that I had filled at Santa Ana has been giving me trouble. As long as I'm on the ground it's ok, but when I'm up stairs at high altitude it just about knocks me out. Today I was in the middle of a lazy eight and it hit me. I thought the whole side of my face was knocked off. I just cut the gun and dove it straight down. Pulled out at 2300 feet and it stopped hurting immediately. From 3000 feet down to the ground it's ok, but above that it paralyzes me. I'm gonna try it again tomorrow and if it keeps on I'll have to go out and have it yanked. I hate to lose it though.

Well, I spent a couple of days on the beach this weekend. We called the Big Bear trip off till later. Got a little tan too, and a good time was had by all. The new class (lower classman) came in yesterday and we've got them scared to move. A few of my buddies that were held over at Santa Ana came in with them.

Got a letter from Aunt Ethel, HG, and Warren Pendergraph today. Aunt Ethel said you all had a grand Easter together. HG says he just sleeps all day and works all night. Pendergraph was a mess. Still making all the money he can.I haven't done much writing for the last two weeks and I got a stack of letters to answer, so I'd better start winding this thing up so I can drop a few lines to the others before I hit the sack.

Take it easy all of you and don't forget that little prayer for me. This stuff is getting rougher every day and I've still got a good ways to go. I've just got to make it. Write soon and stay happy.

Love and kisses,

J

April 21, 1944

Hello good people,

I really haven't much news for you today. I'm still sweating it out and trying to make every day count. Was at fly in formation again this afternoon and it's loads of fun. Works you to death, at least it did me this afternoon. Mostly due to a 30 mph wind.

Been getting your letters OK and they mean a lot. Papers are coming in OK but there seems to be very little news about anybody I know.

I got a new instructor now, my old one is working with the new class that just came in. This one I got now seems to be a good Joe.

I got a piggyback ride all lined up in a P-38 Sunday over here at the Ontario Air Base. I'll let you know how it feels to ride a really hot ship.

Well I better sign off now, shave and study a little navigation. We have a big test in that tomorrow. Take it easy, keep writing and don't forget that little prayer for me. I really need all the help I can get now.

Love and kisses

J———

April 26, 1944

Hello again,

It's me and I guess you've been wondering why I haven't written so often for the past week. Well it's this way, things are really getting rough here and I'm afraid for the next three weeks I'll do plenty of sweating. I was scheduled for an army check last Saturday but they didn't get around to me. Here it is Tuesday and I still haven't had it and I've been flying formation all week without having a chance to practice up on my transition for the check. I'll probably get it tomorrow. I'm just gonna do my best and fly the thing as if he wasn't even in there. I'll tell you the boys are really doing some tall worrying. If I make it through this week I'll start night and instruments Monday.

The dentist checked my teeth yesterday and said mine was in top condition. I didn't tell him about the one that's been giving me trouble. I'm hoping and praying that it will soon get better and maybe quit.

How are things at home? You know every time this business gets me down, I sure do want to go home. That's the way it goes, one week you're in the pink and the next week you lose 10 lbs.

I didn't do much this past weekend. I kinda get tired of knocking myself out every weekend. Then if I don't get out of here, I think I've wasted a weekend. I was just thinking, I guess you all have a pretty hard time trying to make out my letters, but

I write just like I feel and think, which is none too interesting, I know. Then, I'm always griping and I guess you can't figure that out either.

Looks like you've had quite a bit of company the last two weeks. The Ingram's, Neathery's, and Peck's. Betty Peck surprises me, coming down all the way from Washington.

Well, I've really talked myself out and haven't said much. I hope I can have plenty of good news for you the next time. Take things easy now and keep saying that little prayer for me. They say if you pray for something long enough and hard enough, you'll get it.

Good night all,

J————-

April 27, 1944

Greetings folks,

From the heart of sunny California where it's raining like the devil at the present moment. We reported to the flightline this morning at 7 AM as usual, but the field was closed in tight so we're in for a little sack time.

I am through flying until Monday when we start instruments. I finished up formation yesterday and took my long dreaded transition army check. I didn't have much trouble with the check ride. It's all in how the check pilot feels that particular day whether you pass or not. You can be the hottest pilot on the field and they can always find something wrong with your flying. This instrument flying seems to be giving the boys plenty of trouble and has washed a good many out. Of course I'm sweating it out.

Since some of us are through until Monday, we'll probably get a nice long pass this weekend. I guess I'll go down to Long Beach and get my watch. I had the face refinished and a fancy crystal put on it. I can't do much more than that because my pocketbook is bare and payday is not till the first of the week.

Well that's about the works. I can't think of anything else that would be of any interest so I'll close now, and trip over to the Canteen for a milkshake. Let's keep hoping!

Love,

J———

May 1, 1944

Hello everybody,

Thought I'd better drop you all a line tonight because I doubt if I'll be able to write again until at least next Sunday. I start instruments and night flying tomorrow and I'll be on the jump from 6:00 AM to 1:00 at night. Of course we're all scared stiff after the beating the other boys took for the last two weeks. 25 of our squadron were in the last bunch and I think 5 washed out of the 25. I'm going to stick with it and do the very best I can. If I do, I should make it. Just keep sweating and praying along with me.

Well, I had a pretty nice weekend. We had dates Saturday night and went dancing out at the Sycamore. It's a nice joint and we had a good time. Couldn't put it on too much though because most of us were nearly broke. Tomorrow's payday though and will all be sitting back on the top of the world.

My buddy sitting across here from me, did I ever tell you about him? He's a slow South Carolinian. I call him my shadow. He doesn't say much. He goes everywhere I go, does everything I do, eats and smokes when I do. Well, I said he's my shadow. He tickles me and then he gets on my nerves sometimes. There's really some characters in this army.

Can you imagine, I've only got two more working weeks here, two weeks and then advanced, if I'm lucky. These next two are going to be the toughest I think I'll ever have to go through.

That's nice to think about, isn't it? We'll go into sun tans tomorrow. Everything is happening tomorrow isn't it? I've got mine cleaned and ready but three pairs of my pants are too little for me. I was just thinking today that if everything works out OK, I'll never have to put those G.I. winter OD's on again as long as I live. I hope to the Lord that I've worn them for the last time today.

I got two letters from you yesterday. Hope I get another tomorrow. I'll let letters pile up on me then I answer them all at once. That's the way I get my mail, all at once.

Well I better quit now then hit the sack. Tomorrow is the day—Wow! Take it easy all of you and if you don't mind, how about helping me sweat out these next two weeks. They won't have a chance against all of us, will they?

Night night,

J——-

May 9, 1944

Dear Mom,

I guess you've wondered why I haven't been writing so often or did I tell you that I'd be pretty well tied up for a while.

Got a letter from you all yesterday and it looks like everybody is well. They're really got me stepping around here now and I sure will be glad when I get through. The weather has been holding us up though and we are a little behind schedule now, which means when the weather does break we will fly our twats off.

My weekend was messed up this week. I had to fly Saturday and Saturday night, so I wasn't feeling any too energetic Sunday. I did go into town and pat the streets for a while.

I finally figured out the picture you got recently. When I was in Phoenix one Saturday, I was waiting to get a package wrapped there in one of the department stores and the studio drug me in for a free picture. I told them if it comes out OK to just send it home. I didn't have the slightest idea that they would ever develop it.

I got a few pictures they made of us here that I'll send you when I have time. I send all of the pictures home so you'll just have to bear with me. I am sensitive as the devil about having my face strung all over the town. The gals, I guess will just stick me up along with the rest of the suckers.

Some of the boys who took instruments with the first batch finished up and got furloughs. They're pretty nice here about things like that. I missed my chance though so I'm stuck.

Well, I better quit the chatter now and see what I can do about getting something to eat. Take things easy and let's all keep our fingers crossed.

Love and kisses,

Western Union Telegram
May 18, 1944

Got through OK shipping to advanced next week New Mexico

Off on 3 day celebration now will write details soon

Johnny

"Three down, One to go! Keep me Flying!"

MAY 29 - JULY 18, 1944

FORT SUMNER, NM
ADVANCED TRAINING

AT-17 (Bamboo Bomber)

May 29, 1944

Hello Folks,

Guess you've been wondering what in the world happened to me. I did write a few lines in with the picture I sent you right before I left California. Did you get the stuff OK?

Tell you the truth, I've been a little down hearted and disappointed since I've been here and just didn't feel like writing. You see, we all put in for fighters, P-38's, and also B-25's. Well, we got down here and this is really a hole and on top of that they tell us if we graduate we will probably go into heavies, Bombers! Well, I could have cried when they said that, but since then we've got in another bunch from Maranna and they had asked for the same thing so we've all got hopes that maybe we will get a break. I sure hope so.

Folks, this is the last sweat. 62 days of it and our dreams will come true. We've got a big calendar up in the barracks and we mark off each day. There is still a lot of sweating to do. For instance, about half the class will be made flight officers. Get little blue bars instead of gold. No difference in pay and stuff from a second lieutenant but, well I'll explain it to you when I get home. Most of us have bought some of our officers' uniforms. I've got a few things myself. Every night we all dress up and then strut around the barracks saluting each other.

We filled out our officers records the other day and had our pictures taken as a second lieutenant. What looked so good to me was the nameplate - 2nd Lt. John H. Ingram A-C. Sounds good, doesn't it? We're flying twin engine AT-17's out here. Nice ships but I sure would've liked to have gotten hold of an AT-6. It's hard to take I admit but that's the way the army does things. You asked for one thing and you get the very opposite. I figure the only thing to do is to just make the best of it and keep on digging and that's what I'll have to do. I was called out to headquarters this morning by our tact officer and was appointed a cadet flight Lieutenant. I don't know how they ever pick me out of all the guys.

There's absolutely no where to go on weekends out here. Lubbock Texas is 120 miles east of here. I'm thinking about making a trip over there before long and see some of the friends I made while I was at Texas Tech. Graduation day is set for August 4. I don't guess y'all will be able to make it down here, besides it wouldn't be wise to come anyway. You couldn't get a place to stay within 100 miles from here. I hope to be on my way home within 24 hours after graduation.

Well, I better close now and follow the squadron out for a chow. You people take care of yourself. Keep on pulling and praying for me and I'll see you soon. Have my paper sent down here.

Love and kisses

J—

May 31, 1944

Hello Folks,

They had something cooked up for us to do tonight and it rained so they called it off. Thought I better write you a few lines while I got the time.

We've about settled down here and I don't think it's going to be too bad. Because there's nothing to do when we get out but we don't get out often enough to be worrying about that. We've been flying now for two days. My instructor seems to be a pretty good Joe. I don't know how he'll be this time next week though. I hope he's not the chewing kind. That makes it hard on me. We're all still pretty sad because they gave us such a raw deal but I guess we will learn to like this AT-17. I sure hope and pray they don't put me in heavies if I get through. There's a lot of worry and work to be done here.

How is everybody there at home? Guess Evelyn gets out of school this week. I hope she passed all of her work OK. It sure is going to be good to get home, I hope everything comes out all right for me so I can spend two of the happiest weeks of my life with you people soon. Well that's about all I can think of to tell you tonight. You know most of it already. Just the same old steady grind day after day. I'll close now and write again soon. We're on our last leg now, let's keep on crossing our fingers and saying that little prayer. Please send me that shoe ration stamp back. Got to get me a pair of officer shoes

Love and kisses

J———

June 4, 1944

Hello folks,

I'm just sitting here taking it easy today. Nowhere to go around here on weekends. Besides, I'm trying to save my money for that wonderful trip home soon.

I was thinking this morning, a year ago today at 4:30 o'clock, I raised my right hand and was sworn in the Air Corps. Seems like half a lifetime to me. I sure didn't know what I was getting myself into.

Things went along pretty well this week. I didn't get too much flying time. I hope I can solo out in this crate soon. Time passes faster when you get into the swing of things. We've had a lot of lectures this week but next week it'll be ground school. Those lectures sure do get us all worked up. They get us in there and prep us on what we will do when we graduate, suggest how and the fastest way to get home. They just keep on blowing us up, until all you can think about is graduating and getting home when you should have your mind on flying.

Haven't had a single letter from you all since I've been here and I've been wondering if my first letter ever got to you. Also, have my paper sent down to me because all a fellow has to look forward to here is his mail anyway.

What do you folks do now? About this time of the year we're all used to start thinking who we would go see first. Remember dad used to raise cain because we all wanted to go at the same time. Well, I'll close now and write a buddy in Texas. You folks just keep your fingers crossed and say that little prayer for me and write soon too.

Love and kisses

J

June 5, 1944

Hello folks,

Thought I'd drop you a line here while I got time. We didn't have to fly this weekend so I went over to Clovis with three other guys. We had a pretty good time. I got tied up with the banker's daughter. She's no glamor gal but she's a lot of fun. The main thing is she's got the chips and two cars. We went to church with her this morning. The sermon was good but it was plenty hot. I like to have roasted. I guess I'll go back next weekend if we get any time off. Her old man is a big member of the country club and she wants me to play golf with her next Sunday. I'll probably knock all the balls away and end up caddying.

Well the upper class graduates next week and if things go OK, I'll be an upperclassman. We'll have plenty of airplanes then and we can really get down to work and get in some flying time. The schedule is still rough and we hardly have any time to ourselves. They throw this stuff at us even faster than they did at Santa Anna. If you get it OK, if you don't, tough!

Got a big old letter from you last Friday. Boy I just hope and pray I come through OK. Today was Father's Day. I wish I could have sent dad something. If you remember, 1 year ago today I got my orders to report to Keesler field. Boy, I sure was an eager beaver then.

I better start winding this up now. It's 15 minutes before bed time, 8 o'clock. Got to get up at 4:10 in the morning. You folks take care of yourselves, keep saying that little prayer for me and I'll do all I can to stay on the ball.

Good night, love and kisses,

J——

D-Day

Hello folks,

I'm as tired and sleepy as I can be tonight. We are on one devil of a schedule this week. We get up at 4 AM and go like mad all day. We have to be in bed at 8 PM. The sun is still shining out here at that time.

I guess the whole country is all worked up over the invasion. We took a radio with us to the flightline this morning and all the time we were in the air we had the plane set tuned in to the news. Most of us are afraid we're not going to see action after all this training but I think there will be plenty of it left for us in the South Pacific.

Had a letter from Betty Peck today, the first I have heard from her in about six weeks.

I enjoyed the school program you sent me even though I didn't know many of the people. I like to have fallen over when I read the list of the boys going into service. Those guys in Washington really must be loony to be taking those little kids. Maybe they've grown up though since I left.

Flying is coming along pretty slow so far. I haven't got much time flying. Our instructor hopes to get most of us checked out before the end of this week. The upper class graduates soon and after they get out of here we'll get our belly full of this flying.

Well, I don't know how much more to tell you. Not much happening around here. Maybe I'll be able to call you in a few weeks. Take care of yourselves, let's keep on sweating and write as often as you can.

Love and kisses,

J——

June 15, 1944

Hello folks,

Had to fly all morning and when they did let us off this evening, what did I do, but go out and ride a darn horse all evening. Had a lot of fun though but I bet it won't be so funny in the morning.

Things here are going pretty well because being a lower classman makes it pretty rough for us. They are slow soloing us out. The weather hasn't been any good and besides the instructors are few. I hope and pray I can get soloed out this week and start racking up some time.

Got a letter from you today and things sound good to me. Every time I read one of your letters it puts pressure on me. You seem to be so convinced that I'll make it. I'm convinced to a certain degree but I'd sure feel better if I had a good idea on how things will come out. We all laugh sometimes about how our folks think we are just the tops and are looking for us to come home with wings and bars and how we sweat, work and pray that we won't let them down.

Took an instrument check today. It was pretty darn rough up there today for instruments. Hope I did OK on it.

I was called over to the hospital today and they took more x-rays of my elbow. They aren't in a rush for pilots now as you know and they lay awake at night thinking of some way to hook us. I have to go back in the morning to see the flight surgeon. I think it'll come out OK. I got a perfectly good arm.

I can hardly make sense here. The guys have got their officers' uniforms on again tonight and each one has to ask me 10 times a piece if it's too big here and doesn't fit there. Between you and I they all look funny in them after seeing them for 365 days a year in those GI's.

Folks, I have to quit now and clean up for bed. By the time you get back from chow, it's 8:00 and you have one hour of free time before bed. You have so much to do that you never can crowd it all in those 60 minutes. Folks, let's keep sweating and praying and if the Lord's with me, I'll see you all August 4.

Good night,

J————-

June 23, 1944

Hello folks,

Think I'll drop you a few lines here while everything is quiet. The boys went to the show tonight and for once I can sit down and write without being asked 40 million questions and having to move all over the barracks.

Got a good old long letter from you today. Enjoyed every little word of it. Seems that you folks have been doing fine without me. I know it's hard on you (Ha). I'll answer some of your questions here now. Seems that every time I sit down to write to you I never can find your letters and can't remember some of the things you ask about. It seems that the arm x-ray turned out to be a matter of formality and that was a big relief. I'll be an upperclassman next Monday. Just five more weeks from then on out. They sure are passing awfully slow. We got just two more weeks of ground school and when that's over we will have more time to ourselves. I've got a navigation exam Monday and I got to make good on it. I drew a 68 on the first one. First test I flunked since primary. Got to get on the ball!

The picture you sent looks just like you. Looks like a new Easter outfit you have on. What's that you have on your head, a paper plate? Talk about being hot at home, you should be out here in this desert. They put us to bed at 8 o'clock and the best you can do is to get to sleep by 10, and we're up at 4:10. I get up every morning as tired as I was when I went to bed. They say this temp is just mild, wait till July and August!

Read in the paper yesterday about the bill going through Congress now that will send us to college for free after the war. All tuition free plus $50 a month spending money. I hope I'm not an old man when I get out of this deal so I can take advantage of that. Always wanted to go to college.

Bought me a pair of officer suntans in Clovis last Saturday. How are the stores fixed there with officers' clothes? We can't get anything out here. I hope to get most of my stuff there at home where I can get some nice goods. Saving my money too. I'd like to get myself a car if I don't spend it all on clothes. If I get through this OK, I'll be making $250 a month. I should be able to get a pretty good car on that. I'm always building castles but who knows, they may work out for me. I guess you'll get tired of me talking when I get home and there's 1 million things I'll have to tell you. Lots that I don't have time to write. Yep, it looks like all the kids are marrying up now. Maybe I should when I get my wings. $350 a month if you got a wife. What would I want with one?

J———-------

I wrote Judson Pickert, you know you sent me a clipping out of the paper about him being in Texas. I've got a cross country hop down to his field sometime soon so I wrote to him that I may be able to see him. We'll land there at Big Springs for gas and oil so I hope to get to see him if we lay over long enough. This twin engine isn't so bad. You always have one of your buddies co-piloting for you so it's a lot of fun flying together. Sure would like to have got a single engine AT-6 though. I may stay in this flying business long enough to fly everything the army's got.

Well, looks like I've written a letter here and haven't said a thing. Just bear with me though. Folks, let's keep praying and hoping. I'm going to do all I can toward seeing a safe, sound, and happy Aug. 4th.

Love and kisses,

J———

June 28, 1944

Hello folks,

Got a little time on my hand here so I'll drop you a line of the bull on this outpost. Hope this will make some sense. The guys are playing with "Smokey" our mascot and making a heck of a lot of noise. Smokey is a little kitten we picked up the other day and he's really a mess. We got a little sandbox for him and the guys get a big kick out of watching him use it. Went on a 400 mile cross country today and took him with us. He's a good crew man. I was over Lubbock today and got a big kick over seeing old Texas Tech and the little airfield I flew the Cubs off of.

First couple of days I get off I'm going over and check the town. The upper class graduated today and were they a happy bunch. They got their wings at 11 o'clock this morning and by 11:05 there wasn't one around. They left for home in all directions. 36 more days and I hope and pray I'll be doing the same. They sure were sharp looking in their uniforms.

I just finished plotting another cross country for tomorrow, up to Albuquerque and Las Vegas so I better get to bed now and get a good night's sleep for the trip. I was up for about five hours on a cross country today and I was really whipped when I got back. You good people take things easy and keep on pulling for me. Write as often as you can and I will when I can.

Love and kisses,

J———-

June 30, 1944

    Hello "Good People"

    Got quite a few letters to answer here but every time I sit down to answer them I write to you all first and that's about as far as I get.

    I have put quite a bit of time in so far this week. We've been on cross country hops all week. Was weathered in yesterday evening up in Las Vegas and a bunch of us had to spend last night up there. We had a big time. They sent us out to the army camp near there and most of the guys stationed there haven't been in but a few weeks so we had a time shooting the bull with them about the army and flying. We got up at 5 o'clock this morning and went out to the airfield in trucks, pre-flighted our ships and took off for home. Of course we gave the camp a good buzz job before we headed for home, got in here about 7 o'clock, took a shower and cleaned up and was up the rest of the day. We are going over to Texas again tomorrow. Oh! Yeah Smokey, our kitten was with us last night too. He slept with Ed, my bunkmate.

    Sure did enjoy your letter today. Sounds just like home. We marked another day off our calendar today, 36 more to go. Slow but sure! Got a big fat Sunday paper today and read about lots of people I know. Miss Hobgood looked awfully good. See where an awful lot of little gals got married too.

    That was tough about Ham! getting washed out. I saw him when I was in Santa Ana. He was a couple of classes behind me.

I guess the boys just can't figure out how I got this far. Sometimes I wonder myself! Well that's about all I know for tonight. They got a murder mystery on the radio here and I can't think so good. You folks be good. Let's keep hoping and praying, and I will see you again soon. Write when you can.

Love and kisses,

J———--

July 5, 1944

Hello people,

It does look like I'm kind of letting you folks down about writing, I get about three letters from you to my one. They still keep us hopping though and it's the same old story. I just don't have the time.

Flying is rushing along now. After this week we will be at it night and day. I went to the instrument squadron today and I guess I'll sweat that out for the next seven or eight days. After that it's over I guess and we'll really have fun again. We've been having a lot of fun flying cross country and formation. We had a 15 ship formation the other day. We get a big kick out of that. Especially peeling off at five second intervals from 10,000 feet.

I finish ground school Friday and that sure will be a relief. Got a 96 and 100 on my last two navigation exams. You know I flunked the first one with a 68. Finished up with an 88 average and that made me feel good. They wash us out if we flunk a subject in ground school.

Saw a guy in Clovis from home last Saturday. Evelyn would know him, Bobby Eblen. He's a tail gunner on a B-29. May run into him again before I get out of here.

Yesterday was the fourth and as usual we were up at 3:50 and in the air before daybreak. That evening though we paraded in the rain up and down the blocks of Main Street in Fort Sumner.

The Cowboys and Indians came from miles around and they are really a sight to see. Guess you folks had a quiet one as usual.

I sure did enjoy the pictures. Looks like you've turned the front yard into a country club or something. Nevertheless, you all look about the same. Believe the old man is getting better looking every day. Sure has got a white head of hair, I like it!

The paper is coming in OK and they are lots of help. I just can't believe it when I read about a lot of my old school buddies missing in action. I know you remember Carlyle Council. He used to come over all the time. This darn war is just going too far.

They tell us we will end up in the South Pacific bombing the Japs and it won't be long either. You never can tell what those brass hats will do.

I better sign off now and hit the sack, it's 7:30. Keep your fingers crossed and say that little prayer for me and I'll write again soon.

Love & kisses,

J———

July 10, 1944

Hello folks,

How's every little thing? I'm writing this morning to tell you that I hope to come home by plane and I want to know what you folks think about it. It'll cost me, but I figure every extra day at home will mean more to me than all kinds of money. I've investigated trains, etc,, and found out that it's hard to get connections and besides, I'd be a week getting there. There's not much difference between train and plane fares either. If you remember, I'm way out here in the desert and it seems as though the railroads do very little business this far down and what trains do come through are very slow.

Well, I called Amarillo this morning and arranged a reservation with TWA airlines to Raleigh for the 4th or 5th. That way it will only take a little over 24 hrs. I hope. I'll go from here to Washington DC and then take Eastern Airlines to Raleigh. The fair will be about $100 and I may have to ask for a little help from you. It won't be much and I can pay you back in a month. Understand now it won't be $100 because I am planning on handling most of it myself. I just mentioned it because I may have to ask for something. The quicker I get home the more time I'll have there.

That's the poop. What do you think about it? On second thought, I will have a few hours layover in Washington and maybe I could get to see Uncle Eddie and them. It makes me feel much better to get things lined up so I won't have it all to do on the last day. Well, all that is left now is finishing up these last few weeks here in good style. I'm still in instruments and so far so good. I got to get in about 30 more hours to finish. Let's keep on hoping and praying.

Well, I better stop now and get ready for chow. Believe it or not we eat dinner at 9 o'clock in the morning. How's that? We fly the rest of the day. You good people take things easy and keep your fingers crossed for me. Write to me soon and let me know what you think about the deal.

Love and kisses,

J———

July 18, 1944

Hello folks,

Think I'll drop you a line here while I have time. We are all shined up for Saturday morning inspection but it seems that the lieutenant is sleeping late this a.m.

I got a letter from the airlines the day before yesterday confirming my reservation. Here's the poop they gave me. I leave Amarillo at 5:54 AM on the 5th arriving in Pittsburgh at 3:27 PM, take Penn Central from there at 3:50 and arrive in Washington DC at 5:00 PM. There I got a five hour layover before taking Eastern Airlines to Raleigh getting in there at 11:50. That's a long way around, but if I can make connections it'll only take me about 17 hours to get home. Of course they tell me that I am subject to being kicked off at any time when the need for exercising priorities arises, but in the event of removal, I will get the next plane out. I think I'll hang on to that and just hope I have good luck. My roommate has a train to South Carolina and it's costing him about $80 and he figures on it costing him at least $100 before he gets home so it's just as cheap by plane. Besides, if I do get put off somewhere along the line the airlines will pay all my expenses until I can get another flight out.

— Open Post —

— be back Monday —

Greetings, I just got back from Santa Fe. four of us went up in my roommate's car and spent a rather quiet weekend just sightseeing mostly. It's a very historical old town dating as far back as 1610 and there was lots to see.

Well, our squadron starts night flying tonight so we've got nothing much to do for the rest of the day. We go to the flightline at 8:00 PM and fly till 5 o'clock in the morning. How we will sleep during the day I don't know, it's so darn hot. I guess my twat will be dragging the rest of the week. If we have good weather we should finish night flying this week and then all I'll have left is a few hours of formation left to go. The time seems to be passing pretty fast. We still mark the days off on the calendar.

Well, I better quit now, I've racked my brain for more gossip but it's futile. You folks take things easy and keep on pulling for me. Write soon,

Love and kisses,

J————-

P.S. I'll be calling you sometime during the later part of the week or next and we can get everything straight.

[John earned his wings at Fort Sumner, New Mexico. His parents were unable to come out to pin them on him. He did make it home and celebrate with his family. He made it!]

Invitation to his graduation

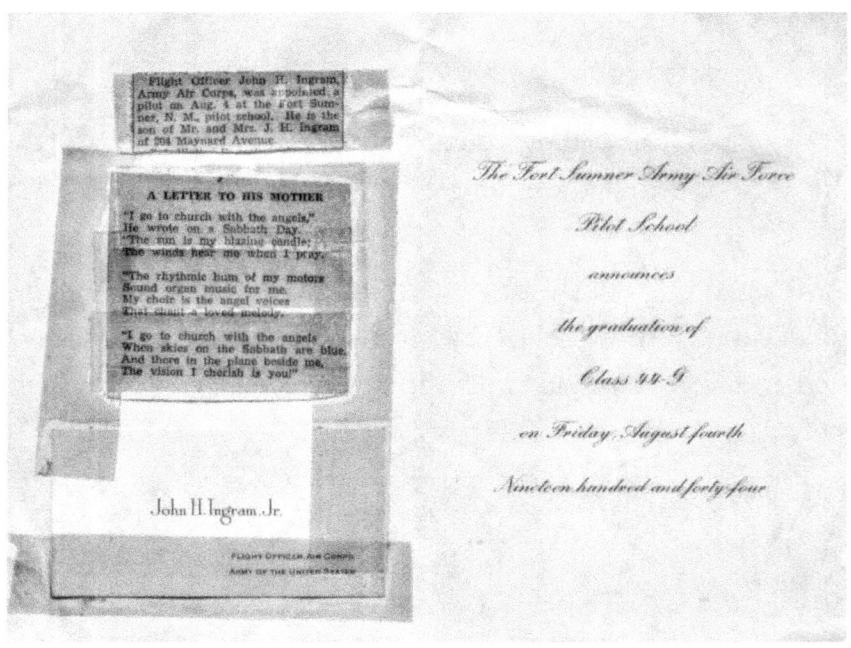

He is a Pilot now! Got his Wings!

First time home since he left for the Service with his Mom and Dad

MADE PILOT—Flight Officer John H. Ingram Jr., son of Mr. and Mrs. J. H. Ingram of 204 Maynard Avenue, was appointed a pilot in the Army Air Forces Aug. 4, at Fort Sumner, N. M., Pilot School. He is a graduate of the 1943 class of Durham High School.

Durham newspaper clipping

The hot shot Pilot in town

John showing off his wings to his sister Evelyn (right) and her friend

August 16 - September 23, 1944
Las Vegas, NV
B-17 Trans School

Air Force photograph
The first Boeing B-17E Flying Fortress arrived at Las Vegas Army Air Field on Aug.
28, 1942. Initially, it was only used for ground training, but by December 1942, B-
17 co-pilots were also being trained as a byproduct of the gunnery training
missions.

Hello Folks,

Well I'm really riding in style and I mean it. I got into Chicago all right and got the sad news that the streamliner I wanted to take wouldn't get me into Las Vegas until 2:40 am Thursday morning and on top of that I wouldn't be able to even get standing space on it. That almost crushed the deal but I decided to hang around and worry them to death until I did get on it. Well, 20 minutes before train time I managed to make a deal with a Colonel that had a compartment on the train and I raced down to get a ticket. The guy handed me a ticket and said $92.99 please. Sounded outrageous to me but I had to make the train so I paid it. Well, I thought my worries were over but after we had pulled out the conductor came around and asked for $40 more and there I sat with $14 in my pocket. So the Colonel agreed to foot the bill and I could pay him later. I don't know anyway that I can wire you from the train so I am wiring you for money when I get to Las Vegas. I hate to do it but I don't see any way around it. The way things look now it'll be a couple of months before I can get back on my feet but those six days at home were more than worth it. I'm hoping things will be OK for me in Las Vegas. Don't worry about me cause old John Ingram will always get along. Take things easy and I'll be home again soon.

Love and kisses,

J——

I owe the Colonel $19.50

August 23, 1944

Hello folks,

How's every little thing? Well, I'm here and they've already got me on the ball and I've got my nose to the rock again. I know I've neglected to wire or write but I've had a pretty hard time getting settled and on top of that we had a lot of crap to go through. They gave me two shots in the arm and for the first two or three days I didn't feel too well. We were divided up into eight sections and the east 4 sections of us are out here in Indian Springs for 2 weeks. So that's where I am now, right out in the middle of the desert again. Was up in a B-17 for the first time today. Flew 2 missions and I think maybe I'll learn to like this big baby. It's a safe old ship anyway.

I hated like the devil to ask you for that money but I just couldn't get around it. Being an officer, every time you turn around they want money for something. Club dues, room bills, etc. I'm a pretty good way from town here so I won't be able to spend much which ought to put me on my feet until the first payday rolls around. We are still on a tight schedule and of course a little ground school and PT, but it's not the old grind that we hit for the last 14 months. When we are not on duty or flying, we are free to go and come as we please and that is something we haven't got used to yet.

Hope you folks are carrying on as ever. I sure had a grand week at home. Nothing much to do but I managed to get around and see everybody. The next leave I get I'll know what to do with my time. If they want to see me they'll have to come out themselves because I'm not going out of the yard. Hope you didn't mind my little idea about going to the station. It's really the best way for me. Enough of that though. The trip out sure drained my pocket. I had no idea it would cost so much. The streamliner I caught out of Chicago and the style I had to ride was what really hit me. I sent the old Colonel the 20 bucks I owed him. He was really a good Joe. I ran into Cotton out here and we had a long talk about the hometown gossip.

Listening to the news right now and it certainly is encouraging. I don't think it'll last much longer, hooray. Well I'll have to stop now. Pretty tired tonight. It's taking a lot of energy to kick that big 17 around and I haven't gotten used to it yet.

You folks be good and keep your chin up. Keep on rooting for me and I'll do my best. Good night all.

Love and kisses,

August 29, 1944

Hello folks,

I guess by now you are ready to come out here and spank my fanny for not writing. I guess I have fallen down on the job a bit but I've learned my lesson. As I said before, our schedules run us through it as a civilian job. We get in our flying and schooling every day and after you're through you are free to do what you want to. Nobody to tell you to go to bed or herd you to chow like a bunch of cattle. So I've been doing more than my share of running around and by now I've seen everything this end of the state has to offer. Been tripping over to the post office every day kind of expecting a line or two from you all. Guess we're back on the pony express line mail and the mail will be slow.

Forgot to mention that I'm still out here at the Springs. It's not so bad. Only thing is that it's a good ways into town and what little gas we get on our car has to be watched. The less trips we make means more money in the pocket .

How are things at home? From the way the news looks now it may be something to that " I'll be home for Christmas" stuff. I think everybody is about fed up with this silly war anyway. By the way, if you'd like to, you can tell the paper office to send me the Herald, I kind of miss it. Got to keep up with the gossip you know. Oh yeah, call Mrs. Hughes, Sam's mother, and get his address for me.

I guess you're pretty busy these days or soon will be, getting Evelyn and LaMarr off to school. Both of them are eager to get started I bet. A few more weeks for me here and I guess I'll be on the move again. I sure hope it's east this time. The boys that just left went to Florida. I got my fingers crossed.

Well, I better quit now and hit the sack. I have to fly the first mission tomorrow morning at 5:30 AM. You folks be good and write as often as you can and I promise to get on the ball and drop you a line more often too. Say a little prayer for me and I'll be writing again soon.

Love and kisses

J———

September 1, 1944

Hello Mom,

I wrote to you folks last night and today I received your first letter. Well, it was so full of news and I enjoyed it so much that I just got to write to you today.

The day is about gone here, all I've got left is a little PT, which isn't so much. Just a quick dip in the pool. Didn't go to town last night but guess I'll have to this evening to pick up some dry cleaning and laundry. It's so darn hot and dusty out here that it's all you can do to make a clean uniform and underwear last you two or three days. In cadets we used to make them last a good week but we're supposed to be officers now and always be on the ball.

So Aunt Ethel was over after I left? Well I'm glad of that. Guess it kind of helped you forget about me leaving, and HG has got the car now. Well I'll give him three or four weeks with it, by that time he will have burnt all of his gas and won't know where to get anymore. We have a time keeping ours running.

I sure got a kick out of the old man going out on that bender. I'd like to have seen that. Someday I'm going to sit down with him and a case of cold beer and see who drinks under the table 1st. That will be something to watch. He was right when he said this is a wide open gambling town. The gambling houses have overcrowded everything. They stay open 24 hours a day and are always full. Most of the guys here were flat broke after the first two days. Somehow I can walk all around those tables and watch for hours and never lay a dollar down. I told the boys they would get a heck of a lot more fun for their money if they would just stroll out on the street corner and throw a handful at a time out in the street and watch the people scramble for it.

Went to the dentist today and he found a small cavity. I am going to have it filled Friday. It's been a year now since I've had them worked on. No matter how much you brush them you still have to have a little something done every once in a while.

Man, I wish you would send me the two pairs of shoes and underwear, and if LaMarr can't wear the hat send it too. Also Sam's address. Well I gotta go now. Just got a few minutes to dress. Be sweet and write when you can. Please send me a set of the pictures we took too. I'll send them right back.

Bye-bye

J———

September 6, 1944

Hi people,

Well, I moved yesterday. Back here on the base now and aside from a pretty rough schedule, I'm doing OK. Things at the Springs were a little lighter with us but that 45 miles into town was pretty rough.

Got two letters from you all today and also one from Sam Hughes. He seems to think he'll be around LA for a while and right now we are trying to work an angle so we can get together. I hope so. Sure did enjoy your letters. Lots and lots of news. Wish I could write to some of the gang but I just don't have the time. It's all I can do to squeeze in a line or two to you folks every once in a while.

I got paid last week and what a fat check but after I worked out my budget it was the same old thing. Looks like it just takes it all. This is the most outrageous town I think I've been in yet. Just a weekend resort town and everybody that comes here has the chips so we get soaked along with them. The trouble is they can afford it and we can't. The cleaners get two dollars to do a uniform, shirt and pants. I sent $100 home Saturday. Thought it was the best thing to do. Most probably will ship out of here before next payday and then if I need any money it won't be so hard to ask you for it .

Well, I better close now and get down to the flightline. Probably some more boresome formation flying today. I'm trying my best to like this box car (B-17). Be good now, write when you can and I'll do the same.

    Love,

    J———.

    Send me my shoes and underwear, and also a set of the pictures.

September 18, 1944

Hello Mom,

I feel like a heel for not writing, but you know me. I don't like to write unless I have plenty of good news. The grind gets pretty boresome and it doesn't make such good letters.

Well, I've held out long enough and I just got to spill the beans. I haven't been writing because I've been on the alert to ship out to Tampa Florida with a 10 day delay in route and it's taking a long time for it to get here. Well, the orders are in now and Lieutenant Sollie told me yesterday that I was on the list and would leave here Saturday the 23rd which is next weekend. I've got my fingers crossed and praying for as many days as I can get and if nothing happens, I'll be seeing you next weekend. Sounds wonderful doesn't it?

I've wired you for $100 to get home on and I'm sweating you out right now. I hope it gets in tomorrow. Well I feel much better now that I've told you. I wasn't going to say anything and just walk in on you but since I had to ask for so much money I thought it best to write and tell you so you wouldn't worry about me running through my dough on these gambling tables or something.

Just all of us keep our fingers crossed and hope things work out all right now and I'll be writing to you more about it next week. Be sweet all of you and I'll see you soon.

Love and kisses,
John Jr.

OCTOBER 18, 1944 - JANUARY 4, 1945

TAMPA, FL
DREW FIELD

A black and white, aerial photo of Drew Field Military Facility in Tampa taken around 1945.

Photo credit: Courtesy of the Special Collections Department, University of South Florida. Digitization provided by the USF Libraries Digitization Center.

"This Photo was taken at the blow out we had before we left Tampa.
The x's, if you can see them, are my crew.
Ball turret gunner is missing.
Had a huge time that night!"

October 18, 1944

Evening folks,

It's a little late for me to be staying up but since I slept half of the day I am not too eager for the sack tonight. Went to the show tonight and had a milkshake at the corner drug store and that's about all. We're still hanging around listening to lectures and taking all kinds of examinations. Some of the guys ship Friday. I don't know when I'll go.

Had a swell weekend. My buddy (Lefty) came over from Lakeland and got me. I spent the weekend at his home and had a swell time. Also went out to see Tommy Fowler, he's in primary out here. We were all together Saturday night. Tommy looks good. He's flying Stearmans, the little ships I flew at Thunderbird. I expect I'll go back over there this weekend.

There's not much to tell about this place. We just lay around and wait for an assignment and dread that grueling schedule will have to hit. From here we go either to Drew, McDill, Avon Park (all in Florida) or Gulfport Mississippi. I don't do much writing. I guess I am just getting too lazy. If I had something to write about I guess it would be different.

We've been having some terrible weather for Florida. There's a couple of hurricanes off the coast and the wind has almost blown my tent away.

How's everybody at home? Fine I hope. LaMarr and Evelyn still get up for school every morning I guess and you and

Sue are probably canning the sunflowers by now. I am stumped
for news now so I better close now and hit the sack. I don't know
what I'm going to do when I get on a regular schedule. I guess
they'll just have to blast me out of bed every morning. You folks
take care of yourselves, I'll do the same. Keep your fingers
crossed and write when you can.

Love and kisses,

J——.

I'll be sending you that money I owe you soon.

Hello Mom,

I just got a couple of letters from you and as usual they were wonderful. It's 12 o'clock noon and I just got in from a morning at ground school. We didn't get off the flightline till 11 o'clock last night. Had to get up and go to ground school this morning and tonight we will fly all night. They say they are cutting out this night flying this week. That will surely be a big help to us. I'm still having a devil of a time trying to find time to write to you folks. I try but I never can get it done. I can call you though but you have to have plenty of time to hang around the phone.

We still work like dogs. The crew is holding up pretty well. Every once in a while I have to jump on one of them for a little thing that they didn't do. I know it seems uneasy to them at the moment but maybe someday in combat they will see how important the little things are. Nevertheless we get along so well and we all gripe together. I was thinking the other day, and I believe I'd be absolutely lost if I were not in the Army. I feel sorry for the 4 F's (HaHa). We've had a cold snap here and it's extra cool here today. The boys are building fires.

I see Dad is still trying to make millions out of that plumbing business, and I actually think that someday he'll have something. I'm having trouble trying to keep my clothes straight. I just about got set up in summer uniforms and now we have gone into winter outfits and I have to start buying again. Things are so darn high for us too.

I haven't got any definite plans for you all for Christmas. We may have a deal coming up. I hope, I hope, I hope. It's being rumored anyway. The train fare sounds outrageous to me. I'll let you know more about it later.

Well, I got up and built myself a fire too. It is actually cold here today. I don't know how much more to write from here. I don't hear a word from the kids at home.

I better quit now and baby my fire along. You folks take things easy, keep them crossed for me and I'll be writing or calling again when I have the time.

So long and write soon, love and kisses.

J——-

November 6, 1944

Hello Mom,

I feel like a heel writing this. I won't try to make any excuses because there is no excuse for me not writing. I have been awful busy though and still am. I got up this a.m. at 6:30 and went to ground school till 10:30. Hit the flight line at 11:25 AM and here it is 11 o'clock tonight and I just got in and had my shower. They keep us plenty darn busy. We have one day off a week but the catch to that is we fly all night the night before so you spend your day off in bed.

Got a good crew and we all get along swell. The boys have been teasing the tail gunner though and he's just getting where he's not scared of the tail. He's just 19 and believes all that crap the other guys tell him. We went down to Cuba today. Flew over Havana. Sure was a beautiful sight to see.

I sent you a package today. I hope you like it and haven't got one already. They seem to be the up and coming style down here. The initials I had put on it will suit you and Evelyn both so you can take turns carrying it.

How is every little thing at home? Fine I guess. I think about you all a lot, no kidding. I don't write anybody anymore. It's hopeless. I've got my fingers crossed for a few days at home when this is over. It looks as though we will get it but you never can tell, so as everything else we are sweating it out.

I've been going to church for the past three Sundays. Trying to get in the habit of it. There's nothing like your own church though.

Well, I better quit now and get to bed. It's 11:30 now and I have to be up at 7:00 in the morning. You folks just take things easy and don't you for one minute worry about your son. I'm in perfect health. Eat and sleep well. Happy as I can be and not a worry in the world. I will always be that way too as long as I know that you're not worrying. Good night everyone. Write when you can and give the world a smile each day.

Love and kisses,

Johnny

Hello folks,

Just a line which I have the time and paper to tell you that I'm OK and that today the crew had a baby. Yep, one of the boys is the father of a 7 pound girl and we're all dishing out cigars today. I think maybe we're gonna name our ship after her if they ever decide on what to name her.

Got your Xmas present yesterday and they look too pretty to sleep in so I just got them hanging on the wall to look at for a few days. Thanks a million and believe me you couldn't have suited me any better. I'm having a heckuva time trying to get cards out to everybody. I think I'll just give up.

Things here are about the same and here's something......
Hold onto your hat! Look for me to spend some glorious days at 204 Maynard Ave.. Can hardly wait but guess I'll have to.

That's about all the news I guess. It's about time for me to eat and hit the flightline. Going down to Cuba again today. Be sweet, say a little prayer for me and I'll be seeing you again soon, love,

Johnny

Hello sweets,

Just got in off the line. Here it is 10:20 and we hit the line today at noon and I've been in the blue ever since. How would you like to spend the day at 20,000 feet? Sounds funny doesn't it?

Got a letter from you today. The one with Uncle Eddie's and HG's in it. Looks like HG is doing a lot of thinking these days. I guess we all do.

Sure did enjoy talking to you the other day. Kind of makes me feel good inside. I called again about two days later but you weren't there. Guess you had gone after the kids at school. I've been doing some Xmas shopping every chance I get. So far I've been able to get you all something except LaMarr. I'm waiting for him to tell me what he wants. I thought he would be the easiest one to buy for but when I got to it I couldn't think of a thing. It's hard for me to get everything done at once since I have to run into town every time I have a couple of hours off and try to do a million and one things. What I'm trying to say is in case all the packages don't arrive before Xmas day don't be disappointed because I'm sending them as fast as I can get the time and I won't leave anybody out. I hope you all will like what I send. I see so little of you and know so little about what you have got and haven't that it sure does put me up a tree when it comes to buying for you.

We here seem to have the Xmas spirit considering the fact that there are no decorations and will be flying on Christmas Eve. The crew and I are having Christmas dinner over at the navigators house. We got to go over tomorrow night and help Margaret, his wife, decorate the tree. Just don't worry about me, I'll make it a big Christmas.

We're still holding our breath for that leave coming up, so far so good. Yep, I had a birthday and as usual it was very uneventful. 20 years sounds outrageous doesn't it? I didn't do much that day. Took my girl to church and that's about all.

Well, here it is 11 o'clock and I was going to try to write HG tonight but I guess I'll have to wait till another time. I have to get in my nine hours of sack time you know. This war is gonna last always.

Tell everybody hello for me. You folks take things easy and write to me when you can and don't forget me in your prayers. Good night and God bless you, love and kisses,

Johnny Jr.

Hello folks,

Just a line while I have the time. Sure was nice to talk to you the other day and I am so glad to hear that the Xmas gifts were OK.

I got the lowdown on our leave this morning and I hope to be home sometime soon, oh happy day. Haven't been doing much here, same old schedule. Spend most of my spare time over at St. Pete dating a little girl over there and she's tops. Got a couple letters from you yesterday. Well, I better get this note in the mail now and trip off to ground school. Got to play with radios the rest of the evening. You folks take things easy now and if nothing happens I'll be eating hot biscuits with you this time next week, love and kisses,

Johnny

JANUARY 1945

COMBAT CREW CENTER
HUNTER FIELD, GA
AND
NEW YORK, NY

Hunter Field Air Force Base

The Queen Elizabeth leaving New York City

Crew

Left to Right (standing)
Johnson - Ball turret - Portland, OR
McGraw - Radio operator - Gaffny, SC
Minge - Arm gunner - Knoxville, TN
Hirsch - Tail gunner - Bronx, NY
Broughton - Engineer - Fort Worth, TX

Left to Right (kneeling)
Herndon - Bombardier - Bluefield, WV
Ingram - Pilot - Durham, NC
Hendrix - Navigator - Columbus, OH
Hines - Pilot - Radford, VA

Hello folks,

Well, reckon I better drop you good people a line and tell you that I arrived here at Hunter field today and now I haven't the slightest idea of how long we will be here. The place is just crammed with combat crews just like us and I keep running into my old buddies at every line. That's about all the news so far as I know about the field but I'll have more for you as soon as things start poppin.

Sure hated to leave Tampa or should I say St. Pete. Patty was sweeter than she's ever been, some girl, cute kid.

I was unable to get my stuff before I left. It hadn't come in yet so I just had them forward it to me up here. So far I am making out without it all right.

How is everything? Same as ever I guess. I sure did enjoy those 12 days at home. Little too restless I guess but I reckon we can allow for that. Tell everybody hello for me and also to write.

That's about all I have for you tonight. Don't forget to send me the picture proofs so I can have a look at them.

Good night, be sweet and say a little prayer for Johnny

Love and kisses,

J——-

Hello folks,

This sure has been a short day for me. I practically slept the clock around today. We're still hanging around waiting for something to happen. Ten crews out of our bunch are already alerted to move out. Don't know about us. I've been trying to get a call through to you, maybe I will soon.

I haven't been into town yet. The guys that have said that it isn't worth the bus fare and so I've been doing all I can to entertain myself here on the base.

Heck, I don't know a thing to write to you except I love you all and I am just as content as the days are long. We are all still together and we manage to enjoy ourselves no matter what we're doing or where we are.

Hope all of you are well and fine. I've gotten over my bad cold or should I say I left it with Patty Cake, (Ha).We've all had a little taste of the GI's. I think it's the water down here. I'm still waiting on my stuff. I'm sure I'll get it soon. I don't worry about it. Waiting to see the picture proofs too.

Well, that's about all for tonight, you folks take it easy and I'll be writing again soon.

Love and kisses,

Johnny

Hello everybody,

Well we're all still sweating the deal out. We did find out something today that really made us moan. We were placed on orders today and here's the way it goes. It seems that we won't fly over after all but will go by boat. We were all looking forward to flying a new ship over but it looks like that is just our luck. We were processed today and will get our combat issue tomorrow. After then I don't know how many days it will be before we ship out of here, (by train of course to New York). All this stuff is strictly hush-hush! So after you've read it just burn this letter and keep the rest of it under your hat OK?

I gotta date with the dentist tomorrow, darn it. I take good care of my teeth but it seems that I can never get by that darn "coal miner" without having something done. A few minor cavities this time. Oh well, I take after my mother. (Ha)

Got a letter from Patty today. She's got it bad and that ain't good. Cute kid.

How's things at home? Same as I left it I guess. I've still got my fingers crossed that I can drop by before long. There is still a slim chance.

Well, that's just about all the nasty rumors that I can dream up tonight. You folks take things easy. I'm fine, well and happy so there's no need for you to worry about me. Say a little prayer for me and I'll be writing again soon, love and kisses,

Johnny——

Hello everybody,

Just got in from town. My second trip in and I believe it gets worse instead of better. The town I mean. I took in a dance tonight given by a girls college here in town. Pretty good dance but nothing extra.

Still here at Hunter Field but don't expect to be here much longer. The latest rumor says we're shipping out this weekend, but this place is nothing but one big rumor in itself.

Y'all be happy to know that my clothes were shipped from Tampa today. I should be getting them anytime soon now. Pretty slow but they will catch up with me.

Got a letter from you today. If it weren't for you and Patty I don't know what I'd do. Sure was good to hear you on the phone the other night. With you folks backing me up, I can't lose. You and what you stand for is well worth all my troubles and I don't mind giving my two bits worth at all. Your "tops" every one of you. I don't like to write sad letters but sometimes I feel like I ought to say just what I feel even if it does make you shed a few tears. Johnny's in there pitching, he's happy, he's ready, and he loves you all.

That's enough for now. I'll be talking to you tomorrow anyway. Keep 'em crossed. Be sweet and I'll write again soon.

As ever,

John H. Jr.

Dear Mom,

Can't understand it, but I sure am worn out tonight. Haven't done anything all day either. Yes, I did get out early this morning and went to church. Fact, the whole crew did. Very impressive service. Everybody knelt at the altar for communion.

I've knocked myself out all day for a three day pass and it got away from me. I was using my lost baggage for an excuse. The leave came through about 2 o'clock, but when I went over to get the final OK, they had canceled the pass. Said they had wired Tampa by telegraph and my stuff had been shipped. So that knocked it in the head for good. All the time I knew that my baggage was sitting up here in the P. O. Yep, it's here all right and now I've got no excuse, oh well.

As yet we don't know when we will be leaving this place. It's pretty definite though, that we will be around 3 or 4 more days. We're still just eating and sleeping.

Got a letter from you today. Mail service is pretty good, keep writing. Darn it, this is just about all the nasty news I know so I'll sign off now till tomorrow night.

Good night all, love you,

John H———

Hello folks,

Just a line to kinda let you know that I am still thinking of you. Wondering how things are going at home and hoping that you're not losing any sleep over me. It's been a fine week here. It was so warm and sunny that we needed a fire only at night. Still no news as to when we move out. The latest rumor though, is Wednesday. Going somewhere in New Jersey. Strictly a rumor.

Sure was good to hear you all over the phone yesterday. I don't like for you to cry though, Mom. I can't help it that I'm in this position. I don't know why but I always feel that I am hurting you when you cry even though you do it because you're happy.

I hope I get the picture soon. I've been thinking of how nice it would be if you could drag the old man down to the studio and make up a couple of prints for me. I'd like a picture of both of you.

We are still doctoring each other's bedsores around here and trying to think of what we can buy next to take over with us. I got myself a good looking short coat the other day. You know I was looking for one when I was home last. And that's about all the crap as to what's going on here. I'm getting your letters OK, so keep writing. You folks just take things easy and I'll let you know if anything comes up. Good night now. Keep 'em crossed and say a little prayer for Johnny,

love J———

Greetings everybody,

Another day here and exactly nothing has happened but maybe I can struggle a little news for you folks.

First, I want to tell you that I now have all my lost baggage in and the clean underwear sure did come in handy. There's a lot of stuff I'll have to send back to you though, mostly suntan uniforms.

How is everybody, fine I hope. Got a lovely letter from you today, also one from "Patty Cake". As you would say, just routine stuff but I like to hear it. Hope you're getting my letters OK. I try to write every night but sometimes I get started and since there is no news I just give up and wait for something to happen.

We're all just sick and tired of this laying around on our cans and are anxious to get moving again, but I guess our story will change a bit once they get us over on the other side of the pond. Of course one can never realize just what it is to be in the real thing, but as for me I'm just waiting to see. I know I'll be back folks, that's one thing you won't have to worry about because I'm not. I got too much to live for and I've got so much faith in my God that I know I'll come through all right. There I go getting all worked up again like my Mom, but nothing to be ashamed of, is it?

I guess LaMarr and Evelyn are still making the 8:30 school bell. Tell them hello for me. I sure get a big kick out of playing big brother to them. I hope I can someday, in the way that I really want to. I kinda wish I was still getting the local paper so I could keep up with the local gossip but I move around so much that it's no use trying it. You'll just have to give me the local news.

I guess that's about all the poop I have for you folks this evening. Honest, there's just about nothing to write about here. Be sweet all of you, write when you can and I'll be talking to you again soon, love and kisses,

Johnny

Dear Mom,

Since I couldn't tell you much on the phone, I'll try to give you the deal here so far as I know. Well, we are leaving in the morning about 7 o'clock by train and the latest rumor is that we're going to New Jersey. The Major told us this morning that if we are not hot, (that means alerted), when we get up there we would be able to get 12 to 24 hour passes out of there so that's why I said that there's a chance to call you again. We're still going by boat. Probably leave from New York City.

All of us seem to be well pleased to get on the move again. See more new country and new sites. Sorry I didn't get to talk to you all tonight but you can tell everyone for me.

I'm gonna be alright now. I'll be a good boy and don't worry about me in the least. The Lord and the government will take care of me. Just keep writing to me at this address and I'll get them all right. I'll write to you every chance they give us.

Guess I better hit the sack now, I have to get up early tomorrow morning. Good night all, keep your fingers crossed for me with a prayer, love you all,

Johnny

Hello folks,

How is every little thing? Thought I'd write to you tonight that I'm OK and still in the good ole USA. The bunch of us were in New York City last night on a pass and we sure had a huge time. Took in all the good spots and heard the best bands in the country, Tommy Dorsey, Louis Armstrong, all of them. Because we didn't get in this morning till breakfast, and I have slept all day, and most of the boys are out again tonight, the barracks are unusually quiet. Oh yeah, I tried to call you all last night and you weren't at home. I'll try again tomorrow night.

I guess Evelyn had a date and the rest of you were out visiting. I hope you have been getting my letters all right. We had mail call here today but I was asleep so I'll probably pick up a letter from you tomorrow. I try to write as often as possible so you won't worry about me. I hope you don't.

I'm still in top shape as far as I know. I feel fine and as you say I do my best day by day. I didn't go to church today. It makes me feel kinda low when I miss my church. There's nothing like your own home church you know. After years and years going to the same church every Sunday it kind of spoils you.

How's Pop making out with his job in Morehead City. Guess it's giving him a fit. I still sweat out his little ups and downs even if I am a long way from home.

Guess that's about all for you tonight. I'm gonna shave now and hit the sack. I'll be getting in touch with you soon. Oh yeah! I may need a little loan too. I hate to ask but I'll pay it all back soon. Good night now, write when you can, and keep them crossed and ask God to take good care of me,

Love,

Johnny

Hello "good people,"

I have about recovered from the little trip now and almost settled in the new place. The base censor gave us a little lecture today and after he got through telling us what we couldn't write there wasn't much left for us to say except that I'm OK and I love you all. I can tell you though, that I am still on the East Coast. I am doing just fine in the best of health and spirit. Hope you folks are all OK. I take it that you are. Geez, I don't know how I'll ever make it. Every time I start to say something it's something I'm not supposed to. Officers censor their own mail so I have to write and censor at the same time.

Did you get my pictures all right? Just mail them to my last address or this one and I guess I'll get them sometime. Hope they turn out OK.

I guess that's about it. Maybe I'll have more for you tomorrow night. I got to hit the sack early tonight. I didn't rest so well last night. The boys had an all night poker game on the bunk next to me.

I'll have to go now but I'll be seeing you again soon. Write as often as you can.

Good night with love, Johnny

Hi Mom -

I have in mind to call you tonight but I'll write you anyway. I haven't been going out very much this past week so I haven't been able to call and I'll bet you stayed at home every night.

Oh I got too hot the other day playing basketball over in the gym and I felt a cold coming on so I started fighting it right off the bat and now I seem to have it under control. Last night I put on two suits of long handles plus all the blankets I could get my hands on and sweated most of it out.

Got a good old long letter from you this morning and also one yesterday. I believe I told you that I got the pictures all right. I sent the smiling one to Patty and the hatless one too. I think they turned out pretty good.

Say, I'm still somewhere on the East Coast but I don't think it can last much longer.

Sounds like everything at home is just so so. Glad to hear that you've got the old man going to church.

Think I'll quit now and grab a bite to eat if I can make it to the PX OK. I ate almost a whole box of ex-lax and it got me running. Good for me though.

Be sweet everybody and I'll be seeing you again soon.

Love & kisses, Johnny

1945

8TH AIR FORCE, 388TH BOMB GROUP, KNETTISHALL, ENGLAND

388th Memorial in Knettishall

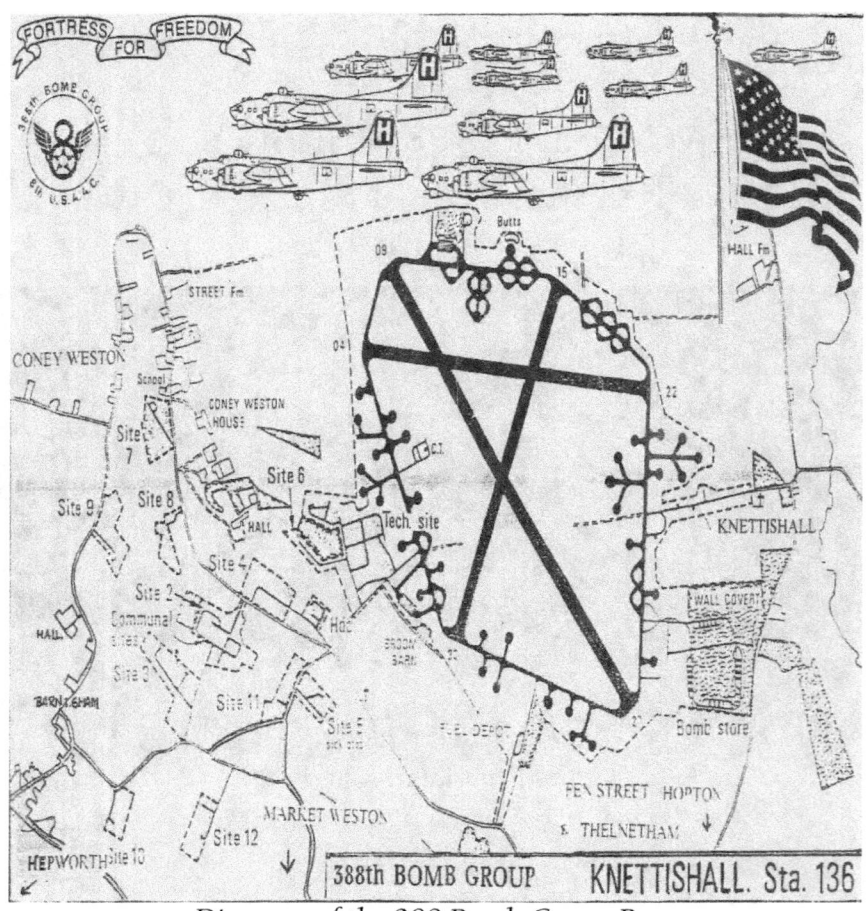

Diagram of the 388 Bomb Group Base

Bicycles were a necessity at the base

The four officers in his crew
He has his .45 on his hip

Ed Hines, pilot of the crew

Feature

I'm Not Superstitious—But Gum, Penny Are Essential Says Flier

LT. J. H. INGRAM

Lt. Ingram Tells Feeling Of Guys Before Air Raid

By ERNESTINE WEST

"I'm not superstitious . . . but I had to have my penny and chewing gum on my bomb runs," sheepishly admitted 2nd Lt. J. H. Ingram, B-29 pilot who has just returned from six months in England.

Lieutenant Ingram, son of Mr. and Mrs. J. H. Ingram of Maynard Avenue, is now spending a 30-day furlough at his home before reporting at Sioux Falls, S. Dak., on July 31. The young veteran of 20 missions over enemy territory was stationed at Knettishall, England, with the 388th Bomb Group of the 8th Air Force.

"The missions weren't as bad as I had expected," he said. He added with a grin, "or maybe I just owe my good luck to my chewing gum."

Article in the Durham newspaper

LUCK CHARMS USED

"You see," he explained, "practically every fellow took some sort of luck charm when he went up. One of the married men used to tie his wife's silk stocking around his neck and my radio operator would prop his wife's picture in front of him. I kept a penny in the heel of my left shoe and never left the field without a stick of gum in my mouth. When I got over enemy territory I stuck my gum on my control column. I don't think I shall ever forget the one time it dropped off.

"We were flying high over our objective, which was Munich that day, when we ran into some heavy flak. We were pretty tense as we always are when we are over our target and there wasn't much kidding around among the crew. I watched my chewing gum drop off my control for the first time on any of my missions. Whether it was a coincidence or the result of altitude, we took our greatest loss since my entrance into the group."

In answer to a question concerning his attitude before taking off on a mission, the young officer said, "You see, we considered it as a job to be done, just as going to an office in the morning or mowing the lawn. All of us would be laying around in the club lounge, smoking and talking about St. Louis or Chicago, and of course, Durham, and we would see a red light flash on the wall. That meant a bomb run the next day. The green light meant there wouldn't be any mission. There would be a momentary pause after a red flash, then a guy who had broken off in the middle of his sentence would begin where he left off. Our work got to be just as routine as a civilian job.

TENSE OVER TARGET

"It was when we were directly over the target that we became tense. Each man had his mind on only one thing and that was his respective job. I suppose that if we had had a pin to drop we could have heard it hit, for we only talked when it was necessary. At the field after a bomb run we relaxed and forgot about it if we hadn't lost any men.

"We had other runs beside our regular bombing flights. We often transferred French political prisoners from Germany. Or chow runs were a lot of fun. On those we would drop food to the Dutch at designated areas. The crew got a big kick out of dropping what they called bundles from 'Heavens Above'.

"Our ship was named 'Heavens Above' by unanimous approval of the crew. Before we went into combat we decided we had to have a name for our plane. We got a folder of pin-up girls' pictures and under each photograph was an appropriate title. Our selection was a blonde with the label of 'Heavens Above'."

Ingram said that the English were nice to them while they were there but that they are much more reserved than Americans. To the inevitable question of English women versus American women, he answered, "American girls just can't be beat."

Article in the Durham newspaper (continued)

1,200 Heavies Hit Reich After 1-Day Nazi Air Bid

The flaming air war which the Luftwaffe rekindled Saturday appeared yesterday to have been extinguished once more by U.S. fighters and bomber gunners as over 1,200 Fortresses and Liberators, protected by approximately 750 fighters, bombed rail yards, airfields and oil targets in central Germany without opposition from enemy planes.

The only air activity along the route of the bombers came in the form of three training planes, which were promptly shot down by the fighters. On Saturday, when the Luftwaffe daringly attacked a force of 1,300 heavies in strong groups, fighters of the 8th downed 64 planes while bomber gunners accounted for 40, making a grand total of 104.

It was the strongest opposition thrown at the bombers since Mar. 2, when fighters and gunners knocked down 73 planes. The renewal of opposition Saturday cost the 8th 22 bombers and three fighters. Ten bombers and one fighter are missing from yesterday's missions.

Visual Bombing Over Targets

The bombers had ideal weather yesterday, with visual bombing prevailing over all targets except a rail yard at Plauen, 40 miles southwest of Chemnitz. The target area stretched from just west of Berlin to 15 miles south of Nuremberg.

Three airfields were hit, one southwest of Dessau and the others southwest and south of Nuremberg. Rail yards beside those at Plauen were at Stendal, 70 miles west of Berlin; at Hof, 15 miles southwest of Plauen; and at Eger, 30 miles southeast of Plauen.

Ordnance depots in the Bayreuth area, 40 miles northeast of Nuremberg, were pounded and another objective in the Nuremberg area was a jet-propelled repair plant at Furth, north of the city. Fifty-five miles west of Berlin, the bombers hit an oil depot at Derben.

Flak, described as meager by airmen, represented the only opposition for the day. One fighter pilot called it a quiet day everywhere in enemy territory, with "not a thing moving."

Heavy bombers of the 15th Air Force made their third consecutive raid on the Brenner Pass route yesterday, besides plastering railroad bridges along the northern Italy front.

900 Heavies Hit Berlin, Hanover Plants

The 8th Air Force aimed twin blows yesterday at Germany's inner circle of war industry and what may be its last remaining industrial trump card when over 400 Fortresses bombed war plants in suburban Berlin and more than 500 ranged over Hanover to hit factories and railroad marshalling yards.

Significantly, ack-ack gunners in Berlin and Hanover yesterday threw up a stiff umbrella of flak, indicating that the Nazis, in expectation of savage attacks yet to come, may not yet have stripped their vital industries in central Germany.

Some fliers over Berlin, where tank, armored vehicle and weapons factories were attacked, reported particularly heavy barrages of ack-ack fire, besides thick clouds, which made bombing by instrument necessary in most cases. Clouds also covered Hanover, where the targets included plants making half-tracks and other armored vehicles.

Some 350 Mustangs shielded the bombers yesterday, but ran into no enemy fighters, a further gauge of the effectiveness of the 8th's and the 15th Air Force's recent saturation assaults on German airfields and plane factories.

Attacks on oil objectives were carried on yesterday by medium bombers of the 9th Air Force, which flew deep into the Reich to strike oil stores southeast of Paderborn and east of Wurzburg. Fighter-bomber pilots reported a general eastward movement of German transport.

Articles in the Durham newspaper
about some of the missions John flew

1,300 8th Heavies Again Blast Reich as Nazis Hide

The air paths of 8th Air Force bombers and fighters were clear of enemy fighters yesterday after Tuesday's destructive raids on jet fighter bases, and over 1,300 heavies and more than 850 fighters carried the 8th's non-stop offensive into its ninth day by striking at airfields, rail targets, ordnance stores and oil objectives in southern Germany.

Heavies Bomb Rail Targets

While fighters of the 8th Air Force had a lean day in continuing their drive on Nazi airfields—early reports last night showed only one plane destroyed on the ground—more than 750 Fortresses and Liberators again swung deep into western Czechoslovakia and southern Germany yesterday to bomb marshalling yards in seven localities ahead of the advancing 3rd Army.

Approximately 600 Thunderbolts and Mustangs went along to cover the heavies and blast fields in the same areas. Whether the Luftwaffe had withdrawn its planes from these fields or had lost what it had in the area was not disclosed. But some enemy craft did appear during the long mission and fighters shot down three.

The marshalling yards attacked, mostly in small localities, were near Prague, Pilsen and Regensburg. Weather was generally clear.

Four bombers and one fighter are missing.

Nearly 1,000 RAF bombers, covered by Mustangs and Spitfires, bombed Heligoland in the afternoon and also struck an airfield on the island of Dune.

Two airfields, five marshalling yards, two oil storage depots, two ordnance depots and an explosives factory were hit. All targets were located in the areas of Munich, Nuremberg and Regensburg.

Latest tabulations of damage wrought by 8th fighters Tuesday show that eight new records were hung up by the Thunderbolts and Mustangs, including the total bag of 305 planes and the 339th Mustang Group's destruction of 100 ships on the ground.

The 56th Thunderbolt Group, leading fighter outfit, became the first group to reach the 900 mark in destruction when it KO'd two in the air and 39 on the ground to boost its total to 904, of which 684 were killed in the air. One squadron of the 339th made a new squadron mark by knocking off 62, and the day's total of 284 blasted on the ground by all groups set a new mark for the 8th in strafing.

Lt. Col. John D. Landers, of Joshua, Tex., established a new individual record in ground kills by getting eight, and Lt. Col. Joseph L. Thury, of St. Paul, Minn., destroyed four to up his ground strafing total to 18½ and lead all 8th fighters in this respect. The 20 jets shot down by the fighters in air combat also created a new record.

Articles in the Durham newspaper about some of the missions John flew (continued)

1,250 Heavies Strike Munich

Heavy bombers of the 8th Air Force once more struck at the source of German air power when over 1,250 Fortresses and Liberators, protected by approximately 750 fighters, hammered ten airfields in the vicinity of Munich, besides attacking an oil depot and explosives stores in the same area.

All the airfields are believed to be bases for jet-propelled fighters, which give the heavies their greatest source of trouble during renewed aerial opposition over last weekend.

It was the third day in a row that the 8th has dispatched more than 1,000 bombers and the second straight day that operations have been facilitated by clear weather. In the last three days the 8th has attacked 27 airfields.

Articles in the Durham newspaper about
some of the missions John flew (continued)

I thought I'd had it on this one.

Note left by John at the bottom of above article

At a pub with friends

Crew photo: John is kneeling, second from the left

John H. Ingram Jr.
Co-pilot in the Hines crew

1945

Hello folks,

I'll give you three guesses, the first two don't count, as to what has happened to me. (Ha). Just wanted to let you know that I have arrived safely and everything is just fine. The trip over was swell for a while until everyone got bored. The food was tops and of course some of our gang got sick.

We have had a heck of a time trying to find something to occupy our minds. We played everything from chess to monopoly and read everything we could get our hands on. Did I tell you what a bang I got from the phone call the other night. I know that it was my last one for a while but I couldn't tell you. I think everyone had that funny little feeling as we watched the Statue of Liberty slide by but just think what a darn good feeling it will be to see her on the trip back.

This is about all I got room for now. You folks keep writing and I'll write to you again as soon as we get settled. Keep 'em crossed and pray, love and kisses

Johnny

1945

Hello everybody,

Guess you've been sweating me out. I mailed you a letter yesterday and I just this minute sent a cablegram so you should have the good word by now that I have arrived safely in England and I am feeling fine.

Haven't heard from you all as yet, but I know that you're writing. Incidentally, if you will use this v-mail I will get the letters twice as fast, OK.

When you have any spare time on hand I wish you would drop by the bank and just kinda check up on my business there and write to me as of how much I have so far, and if it's coming in straight, etc. If any of you want anything now don't hesitate to go down there and draw what you want out. I really mean that now.

I'm really having a huge time seeing this country and it's just like you see it in the movies. I'll sure have a lot to tell you when I get back. By the way, I'll still be glad to get the paper even if it's a couple of months late. Keep your fingers crossed for me and help me pray, love and kisses,

Johnny

1945

Greetings,

I couldn't get all I wanted to tell you on this one little side so I'll just make two letters out of it.

The people over here are very nice. They think the world of us yanks. Riding the train we had a big time throwing candy, cigarettes, and chewing gum to the kids and I mean there were hundreds lined up and down the tracks. They were a little ragged but looked plenty healthy. We are all having a little trouble with this English money though, we just pull out a handful and the guy takes what he wants and leaves us the rest.

How's everybody at home? Write to me all the latest gossip. I am making it OK here in so-called combat. I'm not afraid although I know I'll be scared to death to start with, but I'll get over it.

Have you heard anything from H.G.? Has he got into it over there yet? I've got to get dressed now. Taking in a dance tonight. I'm still holding my own with the women folks. Ha, love and kisses,

Johnny

1945

Hello folks,

I'll drop you a few lines here while I have time, keep the old ball rolling you know.

I probably won't see any mail for at least a month but I know it's there. We managed to keep ourselves pretty well occupied here. See something new and learn something new every day. Have a hard time keeping my clothes clean. Have to do my own washing and dry cleaning.

Had loads of fun at the dance last night. The girls know more G.I. slang, and about our country than we do, so it isn't very hard to get along with them. We haven't seen our ship or heard any of the details but it won't be long now.

Still wondering how dad made out on his exams and also Evelyn. So far I haven't been able to find it necessary to ask for anything from home. I'll close this little note now and see if I can't get this haircut. It's down to my - - - again. Tell everybody hello for me, all of you write and I'll be seeing you again soon, pray, love

Johnny

1945

My dear family,

I just got through bawling out the mail sergeant because I didn't get any mail. I know it's not his fault but I gotta blame it on somebody. I think maybe they have sent it to some other group by mistake. Nevertheless, I'll keep writing so you won't do so much worrying.

I've got me a laundry woman now and I was glad to close that deal. Our base here is in the middle of a little village so we see a lot of the civilians.

We've finished up the indoctrination course and we are now waiting to fly our first mission. The old-timers here have got us scared to death already. I hope we start off with a few milk runs. I'm having a pretty good time here. We were lucky to get in this particular group. It so happens that the 388th has the best living facilities of any other base in the E.T.O. Really is a fine place and we do have a lot of fun.

Are you having the paper sent to me? Also please check on my bank account and give me the details. I've got a little something to straighten out down at the finance department and I need that information.

Well, how is everybody in general? Did dad pass his exam OK? It's a pity we can't use the facilities of a telephone. That's something that I miss. Well I'll close now and beat it up to the line and see if the boys got back OK. You folks keep 'em crossed and sweat these 35 out with me and everything will be roger, and pray too. Love and kisses,

Johnny

I'm in the 8th A.F.

E.T.O.-European Theater of Operation

Milk Run-no flak, no fighters, easy mission, no ships lost

1945

Hello folks,

Been pretty busy the last few days. I am writing every chance I get. I hope by now the cablegram and stuff has relieved the pressure on you. (Ha) The pressure is on me now. Surprisingly, I am really enjoying life in the E.T.O. If it just wasn't for sweating out the missions a guy couldn't ask for anything better.

We have a big party every weekend and they are whoppers. Remind me to tell you about them when I get home. How is everybody? I think of you all a lot. It really works a guy up, like he's been half asleep all his life. Tell everybody hello for me and make them write. I really need some mail. I sometimes feel that I've been forgotten. (Ha). Well, got to get some snacks. Keep'em crossed and ask the good Lord to ride with me and I'll be writing again soon. Good night all, Johnny

1945

Greetings good people,

From the E.T.O. It's Sunday and I've been in school all day. Not as boring as it was in the states though. How was it with y'all today? Guess you went to church this morning and had chicken for dinner. Incidentally, the food here is really good and since there's nothing to eat between meals, I eat like a horse.

So far I really haven't got much to complain about. Had an air raid here last night. I was under the bed, Ha! The boys just came in off a raid and they're taking the roof off the Barracks. We sure get some big laughs after it's all over.

Still haven't received any mail from you yet. Wondering if you are getting anything from me. I'll cut this short and be off for the mess hall. Be sweet everybody and keep them crossed. Write and pray, love and kisses, Johnny

1945

Hi everybody,

Got a few seconds here before I go to chow. We stay pretty busy around here as you can well guess if you've been reading the papers. As of yet, I haven't flown my first mission but it'll happen any day now. Since I've been here I'm pretty well convinced that this business is no joke either.

How is everything around town? Haven't had any mail from you yet but I'm looking forward to it. Our only means of transportation over here is by bicycle and everybody including the C.O. has one. The whole crew cycles now. You should see us.

Have you heard anything from HG? Wonder how he's making out. Write to me all the old poop. Wish you and dad would send me a big picture of the both of you, that would brighten up the soul shack. Guess I'll run along now. You folks be good, take care of yourselves and write when you can. Keep'em crossed and pray for me, I need it. Love Johnny

1945

Folks,

I'll try to stay awake long enough to give you a little poop from the group. The past six or seven days have been a little tight for us. Trying to get ready for our first mission. Probably by the time you receive this I'll have a couple under my belt. Wish I could tell you all the things that happen here. I'll just be plum full when I get back. *

Still haven't heard from you. I am expecting a big stash of news any day now. I hope so much that I'll have to take a day off to read it all.

By the way, if you care to send me something I could use some gum, socks, necktie, toothpaste, cheese crackers, (for the midnight snack ha ha), and whatever you care too. Pack it good because it'll take a beating. Hope you're sending the paper too. Well, that's about my time so I'll hit the sack now. Tell everybody hello for me. Keep 'em crossed and pray that little John will come through. Love and kisses,

Johnny

[his letters are being censored so he could not share specific information]

1945

Dear Mom,

Haven't got much news from you today but I'll write anything to keep up the habit. Still no mail from the states. I think they've messed up again and sent it somewhere else.

We were up for a practice mission yesterday but it was scrubbed. Once we do start flying it'll really be a rugged schedule so there's really no need to be anxious.

The boys are coming in now off a mission. I can hear them over the field now. Won't be long now until they are in here raising the roof about what they tore up today. Some fun, this combat. The Jerrys hit around here last night. We were far enough away to watch the show but we didn't get any of it. Got to go now, tell everybody hello from me and write when you can. Love and kisses,

Johnny

1945

Hi everybody,

It's me again and I'm fine as wine. Thinking of you all as usual and wondering just how the old world is treating you. As for me I am sound as ever. We should have flown our first mission today but didn't. I bet you're wondering when I'm going to stop gabbing about that first trip and hurry up and fly it. Well naturally that is the one thing that takes up most of the space in our numbskulls at the present since we arrived here.

Still no mail from home. I wish those guys would get on the ball and find all that correspondence of mine. What's new around town. Who married who and who is gonna have a baby. I don't know exactly what to write about since there is no mail from you so I'll close now and chew the rag with the boys. Keep'em crossed and pray for us, love

Johnny

1945

Dear Mom,

Your son's morale at the present is at its highest peak of the year. Got up bright and early this a.m., 4 o'clock to be exact, flew one of those dreaded combat missions and I got back this evening very much alive.

I had 12 letters at the P.O. Yep, the first I've received from you since I left. Had a couple from Miss Boland, one from Aunt Beatrice in New York and the rest from you. You just can't imagine what a good feeling it was to hear from you and to top it all, Dad honored me with one from Morehead. He sure has been getting around the country lately. You know I think a lot of that guy.

I hope you have been getting my letters OK. I haven't been writing regularly these past few days because we've been doing a lot of flying. I was plenty scared on that mission today. That's the darndest feeling that could ever happen to anybody. When the going gets rough, I just break out in a cold clammy sweat and well, the feeling just can't be explained. Of course I can't tell you all that happened on the mission but I'll have plenty to spill when I get home. I'm hoping that I'll come out of this a pretty normal guy. Personally, I don't see how those Germans can hold out much longer, the sky was literally covered with planes today.

Home news sounds good. I was glad to hear that Evelyn passed her college exam and I think that Dad got a bad break on his heating exam. The latest poop from the states says that hot weather has already set in at home. Read where it was 91° in North Carolina last week. Tell LaMarr I liked the picture he drew for me. I gave him 100 on it.

So you haven't heard from H.G. yet. I guess he's catching it pretty rough too. I guess that's about all the stuff I can think of tonight. Got to hit the sack early tonight, You never can tell when they'll drag you out of the sack. Tell everybody hello for me. Keep writing and just send me anything you feel like I would like. I am not hard to please. Keep'em crossed and ask God to take care of me. Good night and love,

Johnny

1945

Hello everybody,

Got time here for a few lines before I hit the sack. Just got back from church. I got two more letters from you all today. The mail has been coming pretty good these last couple of days.

I'm sending you a clipping out of the paper, stars and stripes, about the raid I was on the other day. I want you to save it for me. I want to ask you another favor. If you can, would you send off to the Sears and Roebuck Company in Chicago, I think, and get me a (be sure and get this straight) U.S. Army Air Force A-2 type dark brown leather flying jacket. I am pretty sure they are only about $17. That will cover it. I'm positive. The jackets are some rejects from the Army Air Force that the company has bought up. Nevertheless, you can go down to the local Sears company and get the details. I sure would like to have the jacket.

The letter today was full of good news. Looks like the boys are coming back to town and I wouldn't put it past Pendergraft to carry a spit can to that wedding, (Ha). Well, I guess that's about it for tonight. We combat men have gotta get our rest, (Ha). I have a feeling tomorrow will be a rough one. Good night folks. Keep 'em crossed and say that little prayer for Johnny. Love and kisses,

Johnny

1945

Hello folks,

I'll drop you a line here, got to keep up the habit you know. I got three more letters from you today. I hope they keep on coming in that way.

Not much news from me today. I didn't fly today but I guess Sunday will find me up there dodging that flack and kicking that penny in my shoe. Also I stick my wad of chewing gum on the control stick for good luck. Man, I need it.

Thanks for Col. Brann's address. I'm going to write to him. Got to get some poop from him on the other side because we all expect to end up over there sooner or later.

Are you still there at home by yourself? I guess it does get awfully lonesome with everybody away. You should be in this army with all the people and with everything going on, a guy just can't get lonesome.

Today was payday and when I went down to get mine they informed me that I owe Uncle Sam three dollars instead. Yep, I had to pay up my back allotments so that hit me pretty hard but I've got about 20 pounds to last me this month and I don't need it so it's better off in the bank at home. By the way, don't forget to check on it down there and see how much I've got and if it's coming in OK. Ask them to drop me a letter once in a while and let me know how I stand. All I know is that I send it and whether it ever gets there or not I have no way of telling. Also, don't forget my A-2 jacket and stuff.

We have a big blowout here every weekend and I guess the club will be jumping tonight but us combat men will have to hit the sack early.

I will close now and pay my laundry woman a visit. She owes me some socks and underwear. Be good now and write to me when you can. Keep'em crossed,

love Johnny

1945

Easter Greetings to ya folks,

George, my bombardier has gone after the mail at the present, so I'm being a bit optimistic and answering you before I even hear from you.

Got up and went to church this morning. We had a nice crowd and also a swell sermon by the chaplains. Didn't fly today, so last night was a gala occasion, it being payday too. I am wondering if you are getting my letters OK. As yet, I haven't heard anything from you with my new APO #559, but I guess you're gotten it by now.

I bet all of you are in Danville today. You mentioned in one of your letters that you were going over to see Uncle Edgar while he was home. I wrote to H.G. last night. That's about all the news I know today but I'll revisit with you again to see about this money at the bank and also the A-2 flight jacket. By the way, if any of you ever need a few bucks for something, don't hesitate to go down and use that money now. I want you to because I owe you some anyway. I'll write again soon, Keep 'em crossed,

love Johnny

1945

Dear Mom,

I've just about given up all hope of ever getting any mail, but I'll write anyway even though I'm a little lost for news. Today the mission was scrubbed before we got very far. I was full of confidence, but I'll have to admit there were butterflies in my stomach also. Guess we'll go there tomorrow.

I wonder how everything is at home. Hope you all are OK. I'm just fine and dandy and hope it lasts for a long long time. How's dad making out with all his headaches? Has he started the job in Morehead yet? Don't forget to write me everything. I'll run along now. I'll be writing again tomorrow and I hope I can say that I've seen Germany and got back OK. Keep 'em crossed and say a little prayer for me,

love Johnny

1945

Hello folks,

Hey! I'm down here in London town for a little excitement. As you can see there's plenty of going on, me writing letters. Yep! They decided I needed a little rest. Just kidding, you see, this is a treat they give you every once in a while. Well, it's just like you see in the movies. Quaint, antiqueish, with old people running about in silk top hats and taxi cabs that look like they came out of the Smithsonian Institute. I haven't been in town but a few hours so I really haven't begun to see it all yet. As for the bomb damage, they have it all cleaned up but you can readily tell just what a beating these people took over here in the dark days of 40 and 41. I have three days to spend here. My whole crew is out on pass too and I guess most of them came here also. My navigator, Jake, is with me. We sure had a hard night on the train. We had been flying pretty regularly this week so we were pretty well fogged when they came in and told us we were on pass.

I'm sending you a clipping on our mission yesterday. A piece of flak came through the tail yesterday and I thought poor Bob, the tail gunner from New York, was going to have a fit. He started shouting out over the interphone at me that we had got hit and there I was in a dead sweat trying to keep that B-one seven straight and level. When we got back to the base he came running up to the front yelling, skipper we got a flak hole. It was really funny and we all are still laughing about it. You know he was the one that was giving us all the trouble at Drew. Everybody gets scared and excited but Bob shows it a great deal more than the rest. Mail is coming in pretty good now. Sure helps a lot too.

Well, I will get this thing off now and start seeing some of this town. Be good, and I'll write again when I get back.

Love and kisses,

Johnny

1945

Hello Dad,

I got your letter OK from Morehead and sure was glad to hear from you. You sure are getting around lately. Now that you've started that job down there I guess it'll be about like the one you had in Jackson, back-and-forth all the time.

Well, Pop, I'm really in this mess and I'm not kidding. I guess you've been reading in the papers about our mass raids. I wasn't quite as scared today as I was on the one the other day. I believe it was because I was a little braver today and didn't have time to get scared. Combat is not too bad though, living conditions I mean. If it wasn't for sweating out those missions it would be almost as good as the states. Chow is good and I am doing fine. You take care of yourself now and put a penny in your shoe for Jr. cause he sure needs it.

Write again when you can,

love Jr.

1945

Dear Mom,

A note tonight quick before I hit the sack. This British double time sure has me all messed up. Can you imagine going to bed at noon and it's still daylight. Well, we got in our mission today and I'm kind of getting used to it. At least I wasn't shaking as bad today but my flack helmet wouldn't stay on my head.

Got a couple of letters from you today. Guess you took me too seriously about me not getting any mail from here. I didn't realize what a big to do I was making of it. I know you won't forget me. I'm getting a four day pass toward the end of the week and planning on going down to London town for a little whoopy. Keep 'em crossed and take care of yourself, love and kisses,

Johnny

1945

Dear Folks,

Dropping you a line here before I hit the sack to put you in the know that I'm still OK although at times it's doubtful. They fly us till we're dragging and my little butt is so sore I can't hardly sit down. Have been hearing from you pretty regularly and that's good. I sure had a swell time in London. Got your cablegram too.

Have you heard anything more from H.G. I believe I told you that I have written to him. I hope he answers my letter.

Mom, I tried my best to find you a little something in London for your birthday that's coming up this month but everything, even the cotton handkerchiefs are rationed over here and I couldn't get anything, but I'm wishing you the happiest birthday a mom could have and I hope the next one won't find me over here in this mess.

Well, I'll have to toddle along now. It won't be long before they'll be getting us up for briefing. Keep 'em crossed folks and pray lots for me because I need it.

Love and kisses,

Johnny

1945

Dear Folks,

Here it is almost Thursday and I haven't had these flying clothes off since I got back from London last Saturday. Well, I just got down from my 9th one today. I've changed my mind a little about this combat too. I've found out that I didn't exactly know what I was blowing off about when I was home last. (Ha) Nevertheless I guess I'm doing OK.

I've missed getting my mail for the last few days because I didn't get down in time to catch the post office, but I'll be hearing from you soon.

How is everything at home? Same as ever I hope. Guess Dad is back and forth to Morehead city and it won't be long till Evelyn and LaMarr will be getting out of school.

Gosh darn, that's all I can think of at the present folks but I'll be writing again tomorrow. Take good care of yourself and Keep'em crossed for me. Remember me in your prayers.

Love and kisses, Johnny

1945

Hello Everybody,

Well the war situation looks very good tonight and we're all pretty excited when this mess will be over. Today we were to fly our 10th one and the 300th for the group but it was scrubbed at the last minute. Sure was a break for us because it had been going pretty rough for us and we welcomed a day off. Took my laundry up to my laundry lady and she was shocked to see me. Somebody got me mixed up with another guy and told her that I had gotten shot down last Saturday. It was funny in a way and then it wasn't. We have had a little bad luck in our barracks this week and all of us have been kind of down in the dumps.

I haven't had any mail from you the last few days. They come in bunches anyway. I guess you all are still OK and carrying on as usual.

One of my buddies and I went to church tonight. Very good talk by the chaplain. I like him a lot. I lost my bombardier, George, to the lead squadron. They are short of bombardier's over here or something so they took him off the crew and moved him over to another squadron. Well, I guess I better hit the old sack. Got to hit the Hun again tomorrow. (Ha) What am I laughing at?

You folks take it easy, write when you can and Keep 'em crossed for me. Good night, love and kisses,

John H.

1945

My Dear Folks,

With all this noise going on around here I don't know what kind of a job I can do writing, but here it goes with a little poop from the group. I haven't had much time, in fact not any, to write this past week. We came back off of pass Saturday 2 weeks ago and have flown almost every day since. Tomorrow we are stood down for a change and I sure am welcoming the idea.

Well folks, I think my mail is messed up again. I haven't heard a word in 11 days now. Hope something comes soon.

Hey! I got my 13th one in today. So far so good but I can tell you I've never sweated and prayed so much in all my life. I will tell you all about it when I get home.

How's everything at home? Do you get my letters OK and have I ask for more than you can manage to get off. I mean the jacket, toothpaste, stuff like that.

The newspapers have the war almost won over here but I have yet to see any slack in those Jerry's. Just keep on sweating it out with me.

Did I tell you that I heard from Aunt Ethel. I've got to answer her sometime tonight or tomorrow. These guys sit here and fly the day's mission way into the night and what I manage to write doesn't make very good sense to me. It's fun to hash out the excitement after you get back to the barracks but it's all together different when it is going on.

I guess this is about all the griping I can do tonight so I'll close and soak up a little sack. You folks take care of yourselves, write often and say a little prayer for me.

Love and kisses,

Johnny

1945

Howdy Folks,

Well, I waited two weeks but it finally came through, the mail I mean. Got three letters from you. Sure is good to hear that everybody is OK. We were not scheduled for a mission today but I worked just the same. I took one of the new bombardiers up this morning and we dropped some practice bombs. Didn't mind it so much, no flak and fighters you know. Well, I have 14 missions now and if they keep flying like they are now I'll have 35 in before you know it, if I'm lucky.

Tomorrow is your birthday (Mom) isn't it. I tried to find you a little something in London but as you know everything is rationed. Nevertheless, I am wishing you the happiest birthday possible and if there's anything you want or the rest for that matter, use that bank book of mine.

Did I tell you, we got a brand new ship. Sure is a dilly. The crew is knocking themselves out trying to think of a name for it. I've already named #2 engine Q-Ball because it gives me so much trouble, (Ha) Son of a gun conked out on me right over the target the other day.

I guess Evelyn and LaMarr will be getting out of school soon and you'll have more company than you want. Spring is just hitting us over here and everything is budding out. Beautiful site, but it makes everybody more homesick than ever. Are you still planning on the days at Morehead this summer? Hope I can get in on it.

We're due for another pass soon. I think I'll just stick around the base here and take things easy. I may get over to some of the other groups and see a few of the boys I came over with. I guess that's about all the poop I know for today. Think I'll pop over (limy language) to the chow house. I'll be writing again soon. Write when you can, keep 'em crossed and say a little prayer for me.

Love,

Johnny

April 21, 1945

Hello Mom and Folks,

I just finished a letter to Aunt Ethel. Had one from her today and she was awfully worried about H.G. Said his stomach was giving him trouble again and she hadn't heard from him in two weeks. My stomach isn't giving me trouble but those Krauts are. I've got 15 missions in now and the sooner I hit 35 the better. Didn't fly one today. Guess they figure a little rest wouldn't do me any harm. We flew the last 9 straight, maybe that's why.

My crew and I were awarded the air medal with an Oak Leaf cluster today. Sure is a beauty. I'm sending it home to you as soon as I have it engraved.

It's about time for me to get another three day pass. Did I tell you the little laugh the boys had on me on that last pass to London? Well, we were in this place, sort of a club-like and I retired to the john to take a powder. Well, I was standing in this little 2 x 4 place combing my hair when a little blonde came tearing in and said hello and started going through the motions. Well, I didn't know what to do at first but I liked to tore the place down trying to get out of there. (Ha)Everybody had a big laugh. See, the toilets over here are used by both. Just one of the little things that happen every day over here. I get a laugh out of this country and their people.

Don't know much more so I'll quit now. Write as often as you can, keep 'em crossed and pray for me.

Love and kisses, Johnny

1945

Hello Folks,

Oh I gotta make this fast and hit the sack because we're up tomorrow and I have a feeling that it will be plenty early.

Received a couple of letters from you today. One had the pictures in it. Everybody looks the same as ever except I believe LaMarr is losing his teeth. Evelyn looks like summer time. Guess it's plenty warm there now. We haven't been doing too much around here this week. Germany is getting smaller and smaller every day you know.

Glad to hear that you didn't have much trouble getting the stuff off to me. I can't wait till I get that Hot Rock, (Ha), Jacket.

Well the war over here is looking good isn't it? The sooner it's over the better. Well, I'll have to get these lights out before the boys start throwing shoes at me. Sometimes they just reach for their gun and shoot it out. Crazy bunch I mean.

Be sweet everybody, write often and don't forget us all in your prayers.

Love and kisses,

John H

1945

Dearest Family,

My ship came in yesterday. Yep, got five letters from you. Had the biggest time reading them all.

Things here have slowed up considerably. Fact is we're doing almost nothing. Every time we start out on a mission we have to turn around and come back because Patton has marched in and taken the target. As soon as this mess is over we will be moving out. The rumor is back to the states for a while and then the South Pacific. The rumors are flying so thick and fast though, they are more or less just a joke. It's not the missions that were sweating out now it's V-Day.

The guys here are really nuts. They're arguing now as to how often a hen lays an egg. I'm boiling me an egg over the stove here, and that's what started it all.

I bought myself a radio the other day. Sure has brightened up the barracks. Now all the guys hang out down at my end of the barracks and make one big mess right after another. We even got a bicycle repair shop in here and when one guy starts everybody gets the same idea and at this point the place is full of cycle parts and tools.

Glad to hear that everybody is getting along fine. I'm in top shape. I think the lull has helped us all. Kind of put our nerves back in shape. We got pretty bad around here for a while. If somebody slammed the door we all almost jumped out of our pants. Ha. Last night there was a little explosion in the stove, you know how a coal fire will pop, well it did and everybody scattered. We got a big laugh out of it. Nothing to worry about.

Well, I'll close now. My egg is almost done. Thanks for sending me the jacket and stuff. Take it easy and I hope I'll see you before the summer is over.

Write and pray, love and kisses,

John H

1945

Howdy Everybody,

I got a nice hot fire going. Radio is putting out some sweet music and the coffee will be boiling any minute now, Ha. Yep, all the comforts of home. The fire may sound silly but we took off yesterday in a blinding snowstorm. We had about 3 inches yesterday and today it's really cold outside. Last week we were running around here in our shirt sleeves.

We are not doing much now. Looks like it's about over here. I think our bomb dropping days are over in this theater. It's food now to those starving people. From what we hear the folks back home are celebrating the end every two or three days. We will get a two day stand down and that will be one more big party. The main topic of conversation now is when and how we are going home. Lots of rumors but nobody knows anything definite.

How is everybody? Heard from you a few days ago. Looking for my packages any day now. They take a pretty good while getting over here. Well tomorrow is payday and I'll add another 200 bucks to the bank. What am I going to do with all that money? I wrote H.G. about three weeks ago. I hadn't heard from him either but I know he's OK. Don't know any more dirt so I'll close now and write again soon. I got to fly tonight so I'll have to hustle down to the mess hall for early chow. Take care of yourselves, write and pray.

Love and kisses, Johnny

Pay Day, 1945

Greetings Folks,

Been reading about the celebrating you folks have been doing over there. Something to celebrate! Guess it makes sense to get an early start.

Today the wheels informed us that we were through and they expect in a few days the final stand down which means for us to start thinking of getting out of here. Looks awful good. I got a pass coming up. Was supposed to go today but I have to go before the board tomorrow morning so I'll have to wait till Thursday. Yep, they are sending me up before the brass tomorrow and if I can answer all the questions I get a raise in rank. Boy, I hope I make it.

With the radio going full blast I can't do much more writing so I'll close now and stoke up the fire. Be good, write when you can and keep them crossed. It's got to be the states instead of the South Pacific. Wow, are we sweating that deal out.

Love and kisses, John.

(3"of snow today)

1945

Howdy Folks,

Better get off a few letters to you this week. I am going on pass Thursday and I may miss a few days.

Well, I wish the people back in the US could have been on that mission with us today. We dropped food to the starving Dutch people and after you saw that you felt even more bitter towards the Germans. Also you know most of Holland has been flooded and all the people are huddled together on the high grounds. We went in very low, skimming the rooftops and you could almost see the whites of their eyes. They were shouting and waving flags, sheets, and stuff. They were so happy to get it, and it looks like to me they were just simply going crazy.

The Huns agreed not to shoot at us but we could see them standing by their guns. They were motionless at the sight of all those planes. A Paramount news photographer took pictures of the whole mission so if you see it in the news reel, look for ship 309H on the tail, that's me. We got a laugh today at the bombardier, instead of the usual "Bombs Away" it was "Groceries Away", Ha. Really gives us a good feeling to know that we're helping those people and all the fellas say they'll be willing to run a mission like that three times a day.

I haven't received my packages yet. I wish they'd hurry up and come in. Haven't heard much from anyone lately but I have heard from Patty every once in a while and Wanda has written twice, other than that, no one except the family. It doesn't pay to do so much writing.

I guess Evelyn and LaMarr are in the homestretch at school. I hope they both passed everything. I guess I'll be old and gray by the time I get started again.

Well, guess I'll close now and sack it a while. Take it easy, write often and say that little prayer for me.

Love and kisses, Johnny

1945

Howdy Folks,

I'll be taking off on pass here in a few minutes I hope, so I'll drop you a line right quick before I go. Got a couple of letters from you today. Also one from LaMarr, (Ha). Well, we are still feeding those people over there, just this minute we got back. Yesterday they had spelled out "Thanks" in big white letters on the ground. The rumors are still flying thick as to when and what we will do, but none are confirmed as of yet.

I passed (I hope) the board I was telling you about. Boy the questions were challenging. They asked me who the Prime Minister of Russia was. Ha. I hope it comes through quickly. We're trying to get our 1st Lieutenant rank before we go home.

I take it that you are all fine and dandy. Tell you the truth we did have it a little rough here for a while and it had us down for a while but we came through OK.

I'll close now and hit the road. Be good everybody and I'll be writing again soon.

Love and kisses, Johnny

1945

Dearest Folks,

I managed to get back off pass safe and sound but as usual as tired if not more so than I was before I started.

Well, tomorrow is supposed to be that long awaited VE Day. We are taking it rather quietly while everyone else is doing some huge celebrating. We celebrate too every once in a while but it takes so long for everybody to get back into shape again that we can't afford to have that very often. We had a big blowout here last night. I get a bang out of all the brass getting tight and everybody is buddy buddy.

As of yet we've heard nothing but rumors as to what they will do with us. Some of the boys are going home, not me though, since I didn't get to finish my 35 missions. We will just sit tight and hope for the best. I think I will be coming back through the states though.

I guess things at home are pretty well in the pink. Nice spring weather, school getting out and all that stuff. Maybe I'll get in on a little of it. I went down to a nice little resort town on the coast on my pass. Was counting on going swimming but the weather turned bad and I missed my chance. I'm still wondering if you all will spend any time down at Morehead this summer.

Had to leave you for a while (stop this letter), but I'm back. It just came over the radio and everybody is going crazy. Shooting off flares and every gun on the base. We can even hear the people in the nearby village shouting and the whole sky is lit up with layers of all colors. Well, it's too much for me. I'm so tired I can hardly hold my eyes open. We moved over to another barracks today and it about beat me. Good night folks. Hope to see you before long. Happy VE Day.

Love and kisses, John H

1945

Howdy Home Folks,

I don't know much tonight but I'll talk to you for a while anyway. I'm so darn restless and tired of this place that it ain't funny. I wish they would do something with us now that it's done over here. I'm afraid it's going to be another Hunter Field again, just laying around and doing much of nothing but waiting.

Naturally there was a two day celebration here on the base and we really took the joint apart. We've been running some sightseeing tours of Germany as they call them. Taking the ground crews and those men who have been over here for years and never saw Germany. We get a bigger kick out of it than they do too. All the places we bombed and we were so scared and stuff we never got a chance to actually see the damage we did at the time. Boy, it'll take them 100 years to ever get that country into shape again. We came over Paris today so low you could see the whites of the people's eyes. They were having a big parade and naturally this crazy bunch was gonna get into it too, Ha.

I hope by this time my promotion has come through. I'm sweating it out. Well that's about all the poop I can think of at the present. The mail room has been closed since the first of the week but it's open again tomorrow and I hope I'll get a stack from you and also a package. I haven't received them yet.

Folks, you better come on and go with me down to the snack bar for some toast and coffee, wouldn't it be nice though. Well this is it so I'll be seeing you again soon. Keep writing and praying that they won't keep me over here in that occupational force. oooorah. I'll never get home if they do.

Night all,

love John H

1945

Hello Folks,

Got a few minutes here before I hit the sack. I managed to get hold of a couple of sheets the other day and I really enjoyed that sack.

Got a letter from Aunt Ethel today and also one from H.G. and 2 from you. He seemed to be OK but he didn't tell me what he was doing.

We are just piddling around, then fly a little, and go to school. I sure wish they would do something with us. I think I will get some good poop soon.

I'm still sweating my promotion out. Got four or five more days to go. I sure hope and pray that it'll come through.

Well, honestly I don't know another thing so I'll close now. I'll write again tomorrow night. Be sweet and write when you can.

Love, John H

1945

Folks,

Got a letter from you today and the package with the socks and stuff came yesterday.

Well, I don't know much today. We haven't been doing much, dropped a little food and ran a few sightseeing trips over Germany. Other than that nothing exciting has happened. Still wondering what they will do with us.

My promotion is supposed to come through today. I'm sweating it out with fingers crossed.

Honest, I can't think of anything more of any importance so I'll make this a short note. Got to hurry over to the dispensary for a physical, and also have to fly tonight. See you again tomorrow.

Love John H

1945

Howdy Folks,

Same old story, I haven't got much news for you but just wanted to let you know that I am OK. Eating three meals a day and still wondering just what the big shots have up their sleeves for us.

I'm really sweating out that promotion now. They've frozen all promotions on us. One hope I have got is that mine has been in since May 1. Golly, dang, I hope it comes through OK. It's just too close for it to fall through now.

Had a physical exam today and got a shot in the arm too. We've been hauling POW's out of Germany. Very interesting. Only thing is we get deloused along with them which makes things a little miserable.

Haven't heard from you in a couple of days. I am expecting my A2 jacket any day now.

I guess things at home are going as usual with the kids having only a few more weeks of school. Vacation is on the way. I wish I could get Evelyn something for her graduation. I have a nice bracelet here that I'm going to send her. If you can, get her something for me with some of that bank money.

Well, I'll sign off for tonight and hit the sack. Be sweet everybody and write when you can.

Love and kisses, John Jr.

1945

Dear Folks,

I missed a couple of days writing to you. Been pretty busy and doing a lot of flying. They've had us hauling French prisoners of war out of Germany back to Paris. Very interesting but after a while it gets monotonous. Then too, it's such a long haul over and back, and we had to be deloused before and after the trip. You should see those people. Some had been interned for five years and they sure were a happy bunch of fellows. I couldn't understand much of what they said but they grinned, jabbered, and saluted us the whole trip. When we told them they were over France we almost had to hold them in the plane.

Well, I got my A2 jacket OK and thanks a million. Heard from Aunt Ethel yesterday. Said H.G. is doing alright.

We are still up a tree as to what they will do with us; sweating it out.

I hope everything is OK at home. Let's all hope we get to go back there, the states. Got a run now but I'll be writing tomorrow.

Love and kisses, J

1945

Howdy Folks,

I've got a good long celestial navigation mission to fly tonight. Taking off at 10:30 and flying till 5:30 in the morning, so I'll be sleeping all day tomorrow. Might as well drop you some poop so I won't get behind in my writing.

Say, I got a laugh out of the points you and dad figured up for me. I wish the Army air forces couldn't figure it that way. Nope, I'm sorry to say that they gave me about 50 points so you see I have a long way to go. My day will come though.

Well, I got good news for you about my promotion and the way it looks now it should be coming in any day now. You see, I was put in for it a long time ago but the war ended and they froze all promotions just a day before mine was due in, but they've loosened up now and it should be on its way.

Well, we've been doing quite a bit of flying, PW missions, practice and stuff, but tomorrow they are starting an educational program just to keep us busy and I think I will like it. You can pick your subjects. I'm going to take languages and music, piano and saxophone if they have it. I hope they do.

Got a letter from Aunt Ethel yesterday. She writes pretty often. About another week and school will be out. I know the kids are glad. Somehow I haven't grown up yet and I am almost as glad as they are. I get to thinking sometimes that I am not so bad off. All of us gripe and when we were flying combat missions and they pulled up that huge map at the briefing room and said today we're going to hit Hamburg, Hanover, Munich, or whatever it was, you kind of say to yourself, I wonder if it will be today. And when it's all over and you're back on solid ground again, tired and with another mission under your belt, you feel pretty happy over the whole thing. You feel like you have really done something, and I guess it is at that.

Heck, I'm just rattling on here and it probably doesn't make sense to you but maybe I can explain it all to you when I get home.

Did I tell you that I got the jacket OK and thanks a lot. Also a big package of papers today. I'm trying to make my clothes last me without being short of anything.

Think I'll sign off now and see you again tomorrow. Write often and tell everybody hello for me.

Love Johnny

May 25, 1945

Dear Folks,

Well, now that it's over, over here, we can write just about anything we want to. Kind of makes writing a lot easier.

If you have any kind of a map there, find Cambridge or Norwich and I'm stationed just a little southeast of those cities at a little village called Knettishall. This particular section of England is more or less the farming region of the island and the people live in the old English grass thatched roof houses. They are born and raised here and usually die without getting out of a 20 mile radius of their farms. We go to London, 65 miles, on our passes. By the way, I dodged a few buzz bombs down there on our first pass.

When I first got to the base here, I went to the ground school for a week to learn combat radio procedures and general stuff like that. My first mission was to Hanover. When they said Hanover at the briefing room that morning all the fellows started oohing and aahing and there I sat with my mouth hanging open wondering what was going on. It was a rough target and they had been there before. After briefing the Col. called us to the side and gave us a few encouraging words since it was the first for us. Well, I got off the ground that morning and that airplane feels a lot different loaded with 1000 pounders. We were a little nervous and twitchy, but we made the assembly good over France and started out for Germany. Well, I've never seen so darn many airplanes in all my life, we were strung out in groups as far as you could see in front and behind. Well, everything was OK so far as we passed over the lines which were about 20 miles west of the Rhine at that time. I could see the smoke from the hard fighting that was going on down there. A few minutes before our group turned on the bomb run, I got the crew into their flak suits and helmets and had everybody making last minute checks. Then the group leader called for "bomb bay doors open" and we all pulled our ships into good bombing formation and settled down for the bomb run. Up ahead I could see other groups going in and the flak bursting everywhere. Naturally I didn't quite know just what to make of all this so I just held her in the road and followed the rest.

The closer we got to the target the worse the flak got and it wasn't long before it was kicking us around. That stuff looks so harmless until it starts ripping through you. We got our bombs away and were out of it not long after. We turned off the target and headed home. We hit an oil target so I could see huge columns of black smoke coming up. Got home OK and that was my baptism of flying my first combat mission.

We hauled French civilians out of Germany again today. A woman on one of the ships was in labor and she fainted. When the crew got to her one of the French men had tore open a first aid kit. Not being able to read instructions he saw the picture on the iodine showing how to use it on your hand in case of a cut, so there he was painting the woman's hand with iodine trying to bring her to. She didn't have the baby but the boys sure sweated her out. We got a big laugh about the iodine though. Yep! Some good, some bad, that's the way it goes.

About coming home, some days things look good and some days it looks like we might never get off this island, so I don't know what to think. Just wait and see.

Well, folks, this is chapter 1. I'll be writing again tomorrow. There's loads of stuff I can tell you now but I can't say it all at one time so I'll save it for the next one. Good night and say a little prayer that we are headed for the states.

Love and kisses, Johnny

May 28, 1945

Dearest Family,

Well, another day another dollar and we haven't even started home. Everybody's thinking and talking about it but nothing is being done. Inspections, flying, school, and stuff like that. I'm getting a pass Thursday so that will break the monotony. We are going to school now if we want to. They didn't offer any sort of musical program like I'd hoped for so I'm taking psychology and Spanish. Just something to keep us busy.

I don't do too much writing. Still hear from Patty off and on. People can get things so mixed up. I don't know what to write. Did I tell you that I had a few letters from some people thinking I had been shot down. You know when I told you about the laundry lady thinking that I had gone down.

The kids will be out of school in a couple of days. Is Evelyn going to make it OK? I know she will.

Got a letter from you and dad today. It's really an occasion when he writes. How many drunks did you put away while you were on the jury Pop? (Ha)

I'm still sweating out my promotion. I'm about to get disgusted with the whole deal. It would be just my luck for them to lose the papers or something.

Well, I'll close for tonight. Keep 'em crossed and say a little prayer for me. Write often and I will be seeing you again soon.

Love and kisses, Johnny

May 30, 1945

Howdy Folks,

A good good morning to you all. Hope you're feeling tops today. The commanding general is on the base here today and he's giving us a rough time, inspections and stuff. There's a big parade coming up this evening but I think I'll just watch. I sprained my ankle yesterday while playing volleyball and it's one sore ankle.

Will probably go on pass tomorrow for three or four days. I'm just gonna take it easy this time. I spent over my quota last time and I haven't had too much money all month.

Looks like everybody is going home over here but us. I don't mind too much because the sooner we get back the sooner we will hit the Pacific and I'm not too eager for that.

Two days till school's out. Hope I can get in on some of that vacation time. Well I'll close now and go to chow. Be good folks and say that little prayer.

Love and kisses, John H

Pay Day, 1945

Hello Pop,

Got a letter from you and Mom the other day. I know you don't have much time to write but I enjoy your letters when you do.

I flew all night last night. Beautiful night for flying all right. I was way north of here and I believe it or not, it's the first time I ever saw the sun set and rise again in four hours.

Well, the day got off to a bad start. We were taking some enlisted men for a sightseeing trip over Germany and one of my best buddies spun in right near the field. The squadron went into a cloud in formation and when it broke out one ship was gone. We think he spilled his instruments and spun in. I went over to see the wreck, a gruesome sight. You kinda expect stuff like that in combat, but now it hits us kind of hard. Guess that's life.

I am on pass right now but just don't feel like rushing to get started. Guess I'll go down to London town for the three days. I'm having a time with my promotion. They have things all screwed up at division HQ and I'm just hoping they'll hurry and get things straightened out.

Got Evelyn's graduation announcement today. June 7th is kinda late for letting out the school isn't it. I haven't any means of getting a gift or something for her so you just tell her to pick out what she wants and I'll have mother get the money out of my account.

Nobody knows what they'll do with us now. We all have hopes of going home though. Think maybe I'll see you all sometime this summer I hope.

Well, I think I'll quit now and get cleaned up. Might as well get off of this base for a while. May do me a little good. Take things easy Pop. don't let the work get you down and write again when you have time. Tell them all hello for me and I'll drop you a line from London tomorrow. Keep 'em crossed, love,

John Jr.

June 4, 1945

Howdy Folks,

Greetings on my anniversary. Yep! 2 years ago today I was sworn into this Army, Ft. Bragg, remember. I called you from the guard house down there and told you about it. Seems almost like I've been in the army all my life.

Mom has an operation and I don't know anything about it till it's all over. I came back off pass last night and the first letters I opened Dad said you were up walking around and would be home soon. Well, I had to tear the other letters open right away to get everything straight. Glad you're getting along OK. You had me scared there for a bit.

Had a fine time on pass again. Didn't do too much but it was good to get off the base for a while. Oh yeah, when I got back today my promotion was waiting for me!

Things here at the base are happening pretty fast but we can't figure out what they will lead to. Still hoping that we go home though. Most of the flying is still carrying food and POW's.

Well, I guess you have moved down to the beach for a while. I know it will do you some good, all of you. I was also a guy for getting away from the same old grind day in and day out. I hope I can get in on that deal.

Guess that's about all the news I have for you tonight. I got to hurry off to a meeting in a few minutes. Mom, you take good care of yourself and that goes for all of you. Congratulations

Sis! Good night all. Keep them crossed and say that little prayer for John Jr.

Love and kisses,

Johnny

June 5, 1945

Hello Everybody,

A few lines here just to keep in touch with you and to tell you that things look awfully good toward us starting home soon. Just little hints like getting the planes in shape, creating up everything. Rumors of course, and also our mail has been slowed down. things like that give us hope. I think we will be on our way soon, I hope.

Haven't done much today. Was out on the firing range all afternoon. Things are pretty slow here anyway. Bunch of the boys went to the funeral for the crew that spun in last week. I don't go to much for funerals. I just like to remember the boys the way they were last time I saw them.

I don't guess you will go to Morehead until the kids get out of school. For goodness sake now, don't hold up anything on my account. Don't look for me home till you see me coming. I'll close now till tomorrow. Be sweet everybody, keep 'em crossed and I'll write again tomorrow.

Love and kisses,

Johnny

June 6, 1945
          Dear Folks,

          I don't know a thing to talk about tonight. I have done almost nothing today. Went to a class this morning and also got a little poop on how to fly home. Things are looking pretty good folks, nothing definite yet though.

          I haven't heard from you in about four days now. Maybe they've stopped our mail, don't know. I guess tomorrow is a big day for Evelyn. Last day of school and graduating to boot.

          Some of our old buddies that got shot down are coming back to the group now. They look good and sure have some tall tales for us. My roommate down in New Mexico, we came over together, was shot down by a fighter over Hamburg. I learned today that he bailed out OK, but the German civilians hung him when he hit the ground. I know you remember me telling you about my roommate from Texas. John Hughes.

          Are many other fellows coming home now? I should think so. The papers are very slow getting here. I think it would be best if you just stopped them from coming.

          Well, I'll close now. Thanks, I'll take a shower, shave, and hit the sack. I'm not getting my haircut till I get home. Something better happen soon or I'll be in the brig.

          Well I'll say good night now folks. Take care of yourselves and I'll write again soon.
          Love and kisses,
          Johnny

June 25 - Sept, 1945

Bradley Field, CT
And
Sioux Falls, SD

398-5 G 121BU 7AUG45 GENERAL
BRADLEY FIELD,   CONN,

Western Union Telegram
Bradley Field, Conn
June 25, 1945

Back in States

Feelin fine

Furlough soon

Love

Johnny

Feature

Superstitious—But Gu
e Essential Says Flie

LT. J. H. INGRAM

ey
jh
ts

Vhen
dy-
dley
Au-
Ad-
t as
s he

Lt. Ingr
Feeling
Before

By ERNEST
"I'm not su
but I had to
and chewing
bomb runs,"
mitted 2nd Lt
B-29 pilot w
turned from
England.
Lieutenant
Mr. and Mr
of Maynard
spending a
at his home
at Sioux Fa
July 31. Th

England.

Lieutenant Ingram, son of Mr. and Mrs. J. H. Ingram of Maynard Avenue, is now spending a 30-day furlough at his home before reporting at Sioux Falls, S. Dak., on July 31. The young veteran of 20 missions over enemy territory was stationed at Knettishall, England, with the 388th Bomb Group of the 8th Air Force.

Western Union
Sioux Falls, S.D.
August 13, 1945

Arrived here last night, so far so good, write later

Johnny

Wednesday, August 29, 1945
Sioux Falls, S.D.

Howdy Folks,

Wow! It's chilly up here tonight. Guess it's still nice down there. Seemed it turned cool after the rain we had yesterday.

Well, I'm about at my ropes end. I didn't mind it around here until most of my buddies shipped out. Now I can't find much to do. I'm gonna start raising cane around here now to get something done. I'm still sweating out my flying time.

It won't be long I guess. One of these days soon they'll just up and do everything at once (the usual way) and I'll be on my way. I still don't know what I'll do when I get home, but I'll have plenty of time to figure that out. Haven't heard from you in a couple of days. Hope I do tomorrow, in the way of clothes!

Heck! I am wide awake tonight. I sleep till 12 almost every day and when bedtime comes I'm just waking up.

Well, I guess that's about it for tonight. I'll write again soon.

Love and kisses,

J

THE SURRENDER OF JAPAN

"We hereby proclaim the unconditional surrender to the Allied Powers of the Japanese Imperial General Headquarters and of all Japanese armed forces and all armed forces under Japanese control wherever situated."

At 9:04 in the morning on September 2, 1945, aboard the new 45,000-ton battleship *U.S.S. Missouri* and before representatives of nine Allied nations, the Japanese signed the official Instrument of Surrender, prepared by the War Department and approved by President Truman. It set out in eight short paragraphs the complete capitulation of Japan. The surrender of Imperial Japan had been announced by Japanese Emperor Hirohito on August 15, negotiated by a Japanese delegation with Allied commanders in Manila, and formally signed in Tokyo Bay. The hostilities of World War II had come to a close.

Army of the United States

CERTIFICATE OF SERVICE

This is to certify that

JOHN H INGRAM JR 02 022 679 Second Lieutenant

Squadron X 211th Army Air Force Base Unit

honorably served in active Federal Service

in the Army of the United States from

4 June 1943   *to*   25 October 1945

Given at   Seymour Johnson Field North Carolina

on the   25th   *day of*   October   19 45

EARL H KILLGORE
Lieutenant Colonel Air Corps

Finally Home!

Ready to start my new life!

MORE PHOTOS

John loved to go to airshows
John next to a Stearman, he really liked this plane

John studying the schedule

John checking in to the airshow with his son, John Ingram III

John signing the Veteran poster

John Ingram III and Tom Ingram at the 388th Museum at Hillside Farm, Market Weston

John Ingram III (right) and Dave Sarson (left), curator and owner of the museum. Dave passed on June 20, 2021.

The photo they are holding is the B-17 "Heavens Above" leaving the base to go back to the US after the War.

John flew that plane back, so he must be at the controls.

(that photo is also featured on the cover of the book)

ABOUT THE COMPILER, TOM INGRAM

Free trip allows visit to dad's U.K. base

Tom Ingram of Cedar Park won an all-expenses-paid trip to England. He and his brother will explore the old airbase of their father, a B-17 bomber pilot during World War II. Ingram is wearing the pin and hat of the 8th Air Force, where his dad served with the 388th Bomb Group. HEATHER BONHAM / CEDAR PARK-LEANDER STATESMAN

Travel contest winner Tom Ingram, brother plan to honor their late father, a WWII pilot.

By Heather Bonham
Cedar Park-Leander Statesman

Tom Ingram's entry for a travel contest requested a trip to England to an old, empty beet field that once served as a World War II airbase. He said visiting the field could help shed light on his father's wartime past.

The entry – No. 1,206 out of 2,066 entries – turned out to be a winner. His entry described how John H. Ingram Jr., who flew B-17 bombers while stationed in Knettishall, always wanted to revisit the area. Unfortunately, he said, his father died in December 2008 before making the trip.

This month, Ingram will embark on an all-expenses-paid trip to Knettishall, England, and $2,000 in spending money thanks to the contest by Hilton Garden Inn. Dayna Adelman, a Hilton representative, said Ingram's entry tugged on both the emotional and historical heartstrings.

Ingram wrote: "I would like to go there and to see where my dad lived and honor him for his service and sacrifice. ... Miss you dad. Your son, Tom."

"I did it and then went off and forgot about it," Tom Ingram said of his entry.

For Tom and his brother, John Ingram III, the three-day, two-night trip will serve as both a memorial and a way of honoring their father. While they knew their father well,

the details of his years of military service remain a mystery.

"We asked him questions when we were little," Tom said. "We wanted to know what it was like. But he wouldn't tell us."

The brothers knew their father had a footlocker filled with gear and mementos – but it was always off limits.

"Dad and Mom always told us to never go into it," he said, "and we didn't."

With their father's death, the footlocker is no longer off limits. In the trunk, the siblings discovered old letters their father sent during the war and other items and uniforms from his time as a pilot and serviceman.

In 1943, John H. Ingram Jr. entered the Army Air Corps – a precursor to the Air Force – at 19 years old. After flight school, he became a B-17 bomber pilot. Among missions the crew flew was the bombing of Dresden, Germany, on Valentine's Day in 1945.

"That really bothered him all of his life because so many people were killed," Tom Ingram said, adding that his father never celebrated the honors he received that led to his oak leaf cluster award.

Tom Ingram also remembered how his dad never really enjoyed the attention Veterans Day brought to him.

"During Veterans Day, he would say, 'I was one of the lucky ones. I got to come home. Don't honor me; honor the ones that didn't get to come home.'"

I first started thinking about putting together my dad's book when I got back from the trip I won to visit his base in England in 2012. That trip sparked my interest in my father's involvement in World War II.

This has been a long journey and a labor of love. I hope you find this book to be a testimony for what it took to be a pilot in World War II. I wish my dad was around to see it, but I know he has been with me every step of the way.

Never forget the generation that saved the world! "**Keep them Flying**"

-Thomas Sanders Ingram

FINAL NOTE

John H. Ingram Jr.'s military service in the Army Air Corps started on June 4, 1943 and ended on October 25, 1945. He accomplished his dream of earning his wings and becoming a pilot. He fought for his country and became a member of (as Tom Brokaw calls them) "The Greatest Generation."

He also accomplished another dream, and that was to go to college. He attended the University of North Carolina on the G.I. Bill and is a proud Tar Heel alumnus.

He married Mary Underwood Sanders in 1953 and they had 3 children, John, Tommy, and Betsy. He left his father's plumbing business and moved his family to Texas for a job with Cast Iron Soil Pipe Institute.

Left to right: John Ingram III, Elizabeth "Betsy" Ingram Harris,
Mary Sanders Ingram, John Ingram, Jr., Tom Ingram

Over the years he rarely talked about his experiences in the War. After he retired, through the encouragement of his family, he began going to air shows that featured the aircraft that were used in World War II. He began talking about the planes and he could identify them just by the sound of their engines. People would come up to him to thank him for his service and some would call him a hero, but he would always correct them and say that the heroes were the ones who didn't get to come home.

In one of the air shows he met an original WASP (Women Airforce Service Pilots). They both came to the conclusion that she was pulling targets for him when he was stationed in Tampa, Florida. Here is a picture of them at the air show:

He once stated that he should start talking about his World War II experience because it was his legacy. His health began to deteriorate after his wife died and he was diagnosed with a form of Parkinson's that affected his speech. The discovery of the interview and the letters after he passed away became his legacy.

He flew different B17s when he was stationed in England but one of them was called "Heavens Above." His daughter Betsy remembers a story about this plane. On a business trip to San Antonio, as he was eating breakfast and reading the local paper, as all businessmen did back then, he came across an article about a dedication ceremony of some World War II planes at the parade grounds of Lackland Air Force Base. One of the planes was a B17, and the name of the plane was "Heavens Above."(In an article about him in the Durham, NC newspaper after the war he talked about choosing a name for this new B-17. Here is the piece of that article that talks about this)

> "Our ship was named 'Heavens Above' by unanimous approval of the crew. Before we went into combat we decided we had to have a name for our plane. We got a folder of pin-up girls' pictures and under each photograph was an appropriate title. Our selection was a blonde with the label of 'Heavens Above'."

He drove immediately over to Lackland Air Force Base and got on the parade grounds. And there it was, "Heavens Above." There were no cell phones at this time and he found someone who had a camera. He got them to take a picture of him next to the plane. He gave them his address and asked if they would send him a copy of the picture after they got it developed. He was so proud of that picture he had it framed.

Here is your legacy Dad, you got your book!

Love,

John, Tommy, and Betsy

John Ingram, Jr. and Heaven's Above

Keep Me Flyeing

Love & kissies
John H.